THE WORLD'S GREATEST AIRCRAFT
THE ROLE OF THE FIGHTER & BOMBER

THE WORLD'S GREATEST AIRCRAFT
THE ROLE OF THE FIGHTER & BOMBER

Christopher Chant: edited by Michael J.H. Taylor

Published in 2002 by
Grange Books
An imprint of Grange Books Plc
The Grange
Kingsnorth Industrial Estate
Hoo, nr Rochester
Kent ME3 9ND
www.grangebooks.co.uk

Copyright ©1999, 2002 Regency House Publishing Limited

Photographs on pages 2, 3, 4, 5, 6-7, 8-9 courtesy of Michael J.H. Taylor

All rights reserved. No part of this book may be reproduced in any form or by any electronic or mechanical means including information, storage and retrieval systems, without permission in writing from the publisher.

ISBN 1 84013 466 6

Printed in Hong Kong

Page 2: Two U.S. Marine Corps F/A-18s
Page 3: Two Dassault Mirage F1 upgraded
Right: Dassault Mirage 5
Frontispiece: Boeing B-29A Superfortress

Jet Fighters

Many argue that great progress in combat aircraft performance during World War I came mainly from the development of improved aero engines, with speeds from typically 105 km/h (65 mph) for unarmed reconnaissance aircraft at outbreak of war to over twice that by 1918 for fast fighters and bombers. Yet, by the start of the 1930s, major air forces were taking in new fighters that could only manage 322 km/h (200 mph), although these were followed from 1935 by a new breed of sleek and high-power fighters that raised speed to more than 483 km/h (300 mph). In August 1944 a U.S. Republic XP-47J Thunderbolt proved that a piston-engined fighter could pass the 800 km/h (500 mph) mark. But, by then, RAF and Luftwaffe jets were scoring air victories under combat conditions, proving once again the importance of engine technology in the development of fighters.

To achieve 811 km/h (504 mph) the XP-47J had been specially prepared, even having two guns deleted to save weight. In truth, the fastest operational piston fighters were somewhat slower, making the Luftwaffe's new Me 262 jet the only true over 500 mph fighter in service (with the exception of Germany's equally revolutionary Me 163 Komet rocket-powered interceptor), and thereby a real threat to Allied aircraft involved in continental operations. Fortunately for the Allies, only a small number of the Me 262s built were ever to become fully operational, though if proof was needed of the menace they posed it came with the achievements of unit JV 44, which in just over one month in 1945 managed to destroy some 45 Allied aircraft while keeping only six or so of its many accumulated Me 262s flying at a time. Conversely, many Me 262s were lost in operations, often caught in gunfire as they slowed to attack their heavily defended targets.

Simultaneously, the RAF put its own jet fighter into service, as the Gloster Meteor. Compared with the Me 262, the first Meteors had less engine thrust and offered a much lower speed. But the overall design was very well suited to development and the Mk III version that appeared later in 1944 had more thrust, more fuel and higher performance, while post-war versions approached 965 km/h (600 mph).

Piston fighters generally had their swansong during the Korean War in the early 1950s, the first U.S. air victory coming in June 1950 when a Twin Mustang overcame a North Korean Yak-9, both piston engined. Five months later a U.S.A.F. Lockheed F-80C Shooting Star jet fighter shot down a Chinese MiG-15, thus recording the first ever victory by one jet over another, seemingly sealing the fate of the piston fighters, although it is worth recording that reworked North American F-51D Mustang piston fighters survived in service with a handful of South American countries for counter-insurgency right through the 1970s. But, by the 1950s, the era of the jet fighter had begun in earnest and there was no looking back. The U.S. North American F-100 Super Sabre jet introduced the ability to sustain supersonic flight; in 1958 a Lockheed F-104 Starfighter greatly exceeded 2,000 km/h, and subsequently the Soviet MiG-25 took the speed of a production fighter well beyond 3,000 km/h. The story continues.

Picture: Boeing F/A-18F Super Hornet during aircraft carrier trials on U.S.S. John C. Stennis

MESSERSCHMITT Me 262 SCHWALBE (Germany)

Me 262A-1a Schwalbe

The Me 262 Schwalbe (Swallow) was, alongside the British Gloster Meteor, one of the World's first two operational jet fighters. Because of German indecision whether the Luftwaffe most needed a jet fighter or jet fighter-bomber, and difficulties in engine development, operational deployment was later than might have otherwise been possible; with its clean lines, tricycle landing gear, slightly swept wings and axial-flow turbojets, it was arguably the most advanced fighter to see service in World War II.

Design work was launched in 1938 to meet a specification that called for a fighter powered by two of the new turbojet engines then under development by BMW, and eventually an order was placed for three prototypes powered by the 600-kg (1,323-lb) thrust BMW P-3302 engines. Work on the airframe proceeded more rapidly than development of the engine, so the Me 262 V1 first flew in April 1941 with a single nose-mounted Junkers Jumo 210G piston engine and retractable tailwheel landing gear, a type replaced by tricycle landing gear in later prototypes and all production aircraft. The piston engine was later supplemented by two BMW 003 turbojets, but these proved so unreliable that they were replaced by 840-kg (1852-lb) thrust Junkers 004As in a programme that required some redesign as the Junkers engines were larger and heavier than the BMW units. The first all-jet flight took place on 18 July 1942. The five prototypes were followed by 23 pre-production Me 262A-0s before the Me 262A-1 entered service as the first production variant: the -1a had four 30-mm cannon and the -1b added 24 air-to-air unguided rockets. Operational use of the Schwalbe began in July 1944. Total production of the Me 262 was over 1,400 aircraft, but the majority failed to reach operational status. Variants included the Me 262A-2 Sturmvogel (Stormbird) fighter-bomber, the Me 262A-5 reconnaissance fighter, the Me 262B-1a two-seat conversion trainer and the Me 262B-2 night fighter.

Me 262A-1a

MESSERSCHMITT Me 262A-1a SCHWALBE
Role: Fighter
Crew/Accommodation: One
Power Plant: Two 990 kgp (1,984 lb s.t.) Junkers Jumo-004B turbojets
Dimensions: Span 12.5 m (41.01 ft); length 10.605 m (34.79 ft); wing area 21.68 m² (233.3 sq ft)
Weights: Empty 4,000 kg (8,820 lb); MTOW 6,775 kg (14,938 lb)
Performance: Maximum speed 868 km/h (536 mph) at 7,000 m (22,800 ft) operational ceiling 11,000 m (36,080 ft); range 845 km (524 miles) at 6,000 mm (19,685 ft) cruise altitude
Load: Four 30 mm cannon

Me 262A-1a fighter in post-war Czech service as the S-92

GLOSTER METEOR (United Kingdom)

Meteor NF.Mk 11

The Meteor was the only Allied jet fighter to see combat in World War II, and just pipped the Germans' Me 262 to the title of becoming the world's first operational jet aircraft. Given its experience with the E.28/39, the research type that had been the first British jet aircraft, Gloster was the logical choice to develop a jet fighter especially as this would leave 'fighter companies' such as Hawker and Supermarine free to concentrate on their definitive piston-engined fighters. The G.41 design took shape comparatively quickly. The first of eight prototypes started taxiing trials in July 1942 with 454-kg (1,000-lb) thrust Rover W.2B engines, but it was March 1943 before the fifth machine became the first Meteor to fly, in this instance with 680-kg (1,500-lb) thrust de Havilland H.1 engines.

Trials with a number of engine types and variants slowed development of a production variant, but the 20 Meteor F.Mk Is finally entered service in July 1944 with 771-kg (1,700-lb) thrust Rolls-Royce W.2B/23C Welland I turbojets. The Meteor remained in RAF service until the late 1950s with the Derwent turbojet that was introduced on the second production variant, the Meteor F.Mk III, of which 280 were built, in most cases with the 907-kg (2,000-lb) thrust Rolls-Royce W.2B/37 Derwent I.

The type underwent considerable development in the post-war period when 3,237 were built. The main streams were the Meteor F.Mks 4 and 8 single-seat fighters of which 657 and 1,183 were built with Derwent I and 1633-kg (3,600-lb) thrust Derwent 8s respectively, the Meteor FR.Mk 9 reconnaissance fighter of which 126 were built, the Meteor NF.Mks 11 to 14 radar-equipped night fighters, the Meteor PR.Mk 10 photo-reconnaissance type of which 58 were built, and the Meteor T.Mk 7 two-seat trainer of which 712 were built. Surplus aircraft were often converted into target tugs or target drones.

GLOSTER METEOR F. Mk 8
Role: Fighter
Crew/Accommodation: One
Power Plant: Two 1,723 kgp (3,800 lb s.t.) Rolls-Royce Derwent 9 turbojets
Dimensions: Span 11,33 m (37.16 ft); length 13.59 m (44.58 ft); wing area 32.5 m² (350 sq ft)
Weights: Empty 4,846 kg (10,684 lb); MTOW 7,121 kg (15,700 lb)
Performance: Maximum speed 962 km/h (598 mph) at 3,048 m (10,000 ft); operational ceiling 13,106 m (43,000 ft); endurance 1.2 hours with ventral and wing fuel tanks
Load: Four 20 mm cannon

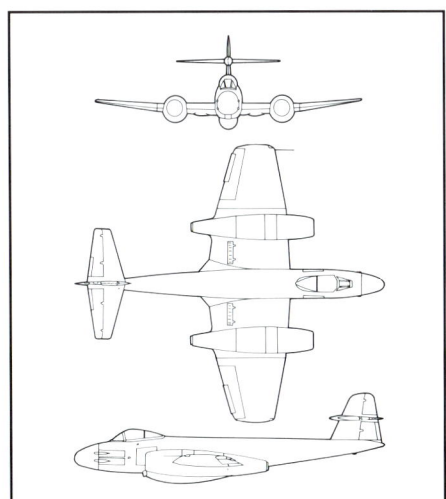

Gloster Meteor F.Mk 8

Gloster Meteor F.Mk 8 fighter

LOCKHEED F-80 SHOOTING STAR and T-33 (U.S.A.)

F-80C Shooting Star

The Shooting Star was the best Allied jet fighter to emerge from World War II, though the type was in fact just too late for combat use in that conflict. The design was launched in June 1943 on the basis of a British turbojet, the 1834-kg (2,460-1b) thrust de Havilland (Halford) H. 1B, and the first XP-80 prototype with this engine flew in January 1944 as a sleek, low-wing monoplane with tricycle landing gear and a 360° vision canopy. The two XP-80As switched to the 1746-kg (3,850-lb) thrust General Electric I-40 (later J33) engine, and this powered all subsequent models. The P-80A version began to enter service in January 1945, and just 45 had been delivered before the end of World War II. Production plans for 5,000 aircraft were then savagely cut, but the development of later versions with markedly improved capabilities meant that as many as 5,691 of the series were finally built.

The baseline fighter was redesignated in the F- (fighter) series after World War II, and variants were the 917 F-80As with the J33-GE-11 engine, the 240 improved F-80Bs with an ejector seat and provision for RATO, and the 749 F-80Cs with 2087- or 2449-kg (4,600- or 5,400-lb) thrust J33-GE-23 or -35 engines and provision for underwing rockets in the ground-attack role. The versatility of the design also resulted in 222 F-14 and later RF-80 photo-reconnaissance aircraft, 5,871 TF-80 (later T-33A) air force and TO-1/2 (later TV-1/2) navy flying trainers that were in numerical terms the most important types by far, 150 T2V SeaStar advanced naval flying trainers with the 2767-kg (6,100-lb) thrust J33-A-24 and a boundary-layer control system, many AT-33A weapons trainers for the export and defence aid programmes, and many other variants.

The P-80B version of the Lockheed Shooting Star

LOCKHEED F-80B SHOOTING STAR
Role: Day fighter
Crew/Accommodation: One
Power Plant: One 2,041 kgp (4,500 lb s.t.) Allison J33-A-21 turbojet
Dimensions: Span 11.81 m (38.75 ft); length 10.49 m (34.42 ft); wing area 22.07 m² (237.6 sq ft)
Weights: Empty 3,709 kg (8,176 lb); MTOW 7,257 kg (16,000 lb)
Performance: Maximum speed 929 km/h (577 mph) at 1,830 m (6,000 ft); operational ceiling 13,870 m (45,500 ft); range 1,270 km (790 miles) without drop tanks
Load: Six .5 inch machine guns

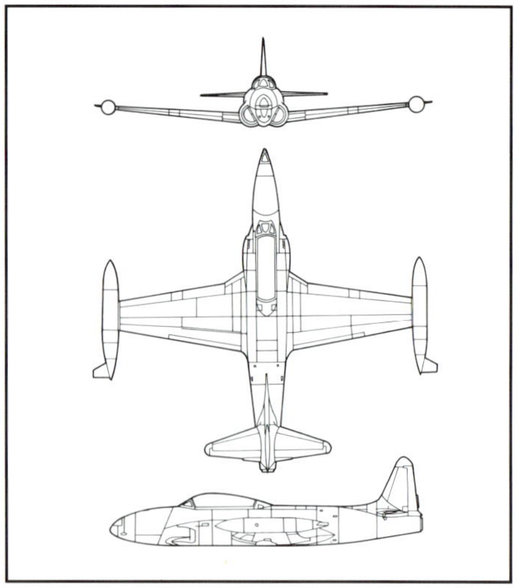

T-33A Shooting Star

de HAVILLAND D.H.100, 113 and 115 VAMPIRES (United Kingdom)

D.H. 115 Vampire T.Mk 11

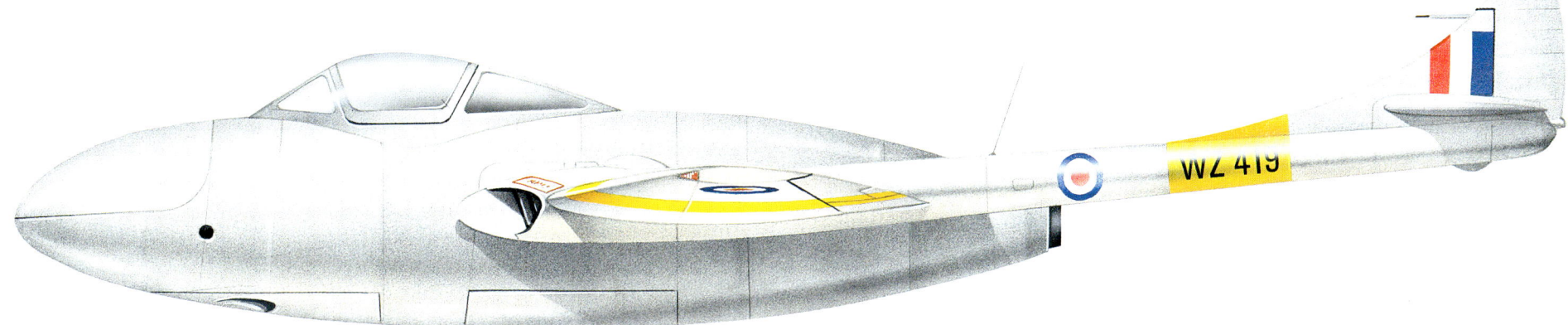

The Vampire, the second turbojet-powered British fighter, was too late for service in World War II. The type, known originally as the Spider Crab, was planned round a portly central nacelle and twin booms to allow the use of a short and therefore less inefficient jetpipe for the de Havilland Goblin engine, which was of the centrifugal-flow type and therefore of greater diameter than axial-flow types.

The first prototype flew in September 1943, a mere 16 months after the start of detail design.

The Vampire F.Mk 1 entered service in 1946 with the 1225-kg (2,700-lb) thrust de Havilland Goblin I turbojet, and was followed by the Vampire F.Mk 3 with provision for underwing stores and modifications to improve longitudinal stability. Next came the Vampire FB.Mk 5 fighter-bomber with a wing of reduced span but greater strength for the carriage of underwing stores, and finally in the single-seat stream the Vampire FB.Mk 9 for tropical service with a cockpit air conditioner. British variants on the Vampire FB.Mk 5 theme were the Sea Vampire FB.Mks 20 and 21 for carrierborne use, while export variants included the generally similar Vampire FB.Mk 6 for Switzerland and a number of Vampire FB.Mk 50 variants with Goblin and Rolls-Royce Nene engines, the latter featuring in the licence-built French version, the Sud-Est S.E.535 Mistral. A side-by-side two-seater for night fighting was also produced as the Vampire NF.Mk 10 (exported as the Vampire NF.Mk 54 to France), and a similar accommodation layout was retained in the Vampire T.Mk 11 and Sea Vampire T.Mk 22 trainers. Australia produced the trainer in Vampire T.Mks 33, 34 and 35 variants, and de Havilland exported the type as the Vampire T.Mk 5.

de HAVILLAND D.H.100 VAMPIRE FB Mk 5
Role: Strike fighter
Crew/Accommodation: One
Power Plant: One 1,420 kgp (3,100 lb s.t.) de Havilland Goblin 2 turbojet
Dimensions: Span 11.6 m (38 ft); length 9.37 m (30.75 ft); wing area 28.7 m² (266 sq ft)
Weights: Empty 3,310 kg (7,253 lb); MTOW 5,600 kg (12,290 lb)
Performance: Maximum speed 861 km/h (535 mph) at 5,791 m (19,000 ft); operational ceiling 12,192 m (40,000 ft); range 1,883 km (1,170 miles) with maximum fuel
Load: Four 20 mm cannon, plus up to 904 kg (2,000 lb) of ordnance

de Havilland Vampire

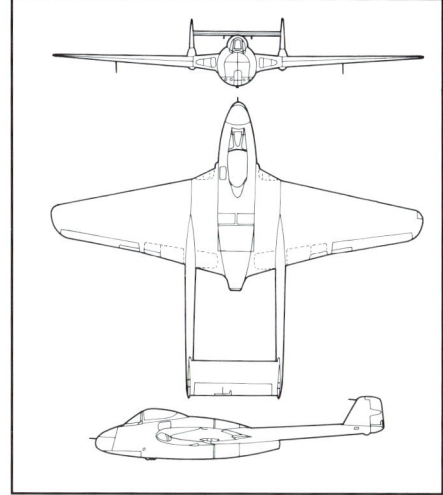

de Havilland Vampire FB.Mk 5

REPUBLIC F-84 Family (U.S.A.)

F-84F Thunderflash

The Thunderjet was Republic's first jet-powered fighter, a straight-winged successor to the P-47 Thunderbolt that first flew in February 1946 as the first of three XP-84 prototypes with the 1701-kg (3,750-lb) thrust General Electric J35-GE-7 turbojet. The 25 YP-84A service trial aircraft switched to the 1814-kg (4,000-lb) thrust Allison J35-A-15, the type chosen for the 226 P-84B initial production aircraft. The 191 P-84C (later F-84C) aircraft had the similarly rated J35-A-13C but a revised electrical system, while the 154 F-84Ds had the 2268-kg (5,000-lb) thrust J35-A-17D engine, revised landing gear and thicker-skinned wings.

Korean War experience resulted in the F-84E, of which 843 were built with a lengthened fuselage, enlarged cockpit and improved systems. The F-84G was similar but powered by the 2540-kg (5,600-lb) thrust J35-A-29, and the 3,025 of this variant were able to deliver nuclear weapons in the tactical strike role. The basic design was then revised as the Thunderstreak to incorporate swept flying surfaces and the more powerful Wright J65 turbojet for significantly higher performance. Some 2,713 such F-84Fs were built, the first 375 with the J65-W-1 and the others with the more powerful 3275-kg (7,220-lb) thrust J65-W-3.

The final development of this tactically important warplane series was the RF-84F Thunderflash reconnaissance variant with the 3538-kg (7,800-lb) thrust J65-W-7 aspirated via root inlets, a modification that left the nose clear for the camera installation.

There were a number of experimental and development variants, the most interesting of these being the GRF-84F (later RF-84K) designed to be carried by the Convair B-36 strategic bomber for aerial launch and recovery.

REPUBLIC F-84B THUNDERJET
Role: Fighter bomber
Crew/Accommodation: One
Power Plant: One 1,814 kgp (4,000 lb s.t.) Allison J35-A-15 turbojet
Dimensions: Span 11.1 m (36.42 ft); length 11.41 m (37.42 ft); wing area 24.15 m² (260 sq ft)
Weights: Empty 4,326 kg (9,538 lb); MTOW 8,931 kg (19,689 lb)
Performance: Maximum speed 945 km/h (587 mph) at 1,219 m (4,000 ft); operational ceiling 12,421 m (40,750 ft); range 2,063 km (1,282 miles)
Load: Six .5 inch machine guns and thirty-two 5 inch rocket projectiles

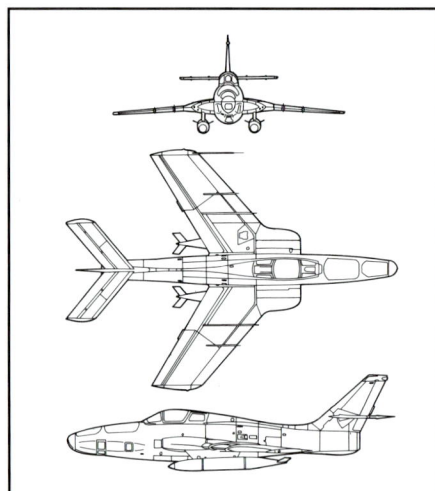

Republic RF-84F Thunderflash

Republic RF-84F Thunderflash reconnaissance aircraft

MIKOYAN-GUREVICH MiG-15 'FAGOT' Family (U.S.S.R.)

Mig-17 'Fresco'

The MiG-15 was the North American F-86 Sabre's main opponent in the Korean War, and was the production version of the I-310 prototype that first flew in late 1947. The MiG-15 was the U.S.S.R.'s first swept-wing fighter to enter large-scale production. The type was powered by the Soviet version of the Rolls-Royce Nene turbojet, which was initially known as the Klimov RD-45 but then in further developed form as the VK-1.

The MiG-15 proved itself a competent fighter, but the type's only major variant, the improved MiG-15bis, could outclimb and out-turn the Sabre in most flight regimes. Many thousands of the series were produced, most of them as standard day fighters, but small numbers as MiG-15P all-weather fighters and MiG-15SB fighter-bombers. The type was given the NATO reporting name 'Fagot', and there was also an important MiG-15UTI tandem-seat advanced and conversion trainer known as the 'Midget'. Licensed production was undertaken in Czechoslovakia and Poland of the S.102 and LIM variants. The MiG-17 'Fresco' was the production version of the I-330 prototype developed to eliminate the MiG-15's tendency to snap-roll into an uncontrollable spin during a high-speed turn. A new wing of 45° rather than 35° sweep was introduced, together with a longer fuselage, a revised tail unit and more power. Several thousand aircraft were delivered from 1952 in variants such as the MiG-17 day fighter, MiG-15F improved day fighter with the VK-1F afterburning engine, MiG-17PF limited all-weather fighter, and MiG-17PFU missile-armed fighter. The type was also built in China, Czechoslovakia, and Poland with the designations J-5 (or export F-5), S.104 and LIM-5/6 respectively.

MIKOYAN-GUREVICH MiG-17PF 'FRESCO-D'
Role: Fighter
Crew/Accommodation: One
Power Plant: One 3,380 kgp (7,452 lb s.t.) Klimov VK/1FA turbojet with reheat
Dimensions: Span 9.63 m (31.59 ft); length 11.26 m (36.94 ft); wing area 22.6 m² (243.26 sq ft)
Weights: Empty 4,182 kg (9,220 lb); MTOW 6,330 kg (13,955 lb)
Performance: Maximum speed 1,074 km/h (667 mph) at 4,000 m (13,123 ft); operational ceiling 15,850 m (52,001 ft); range 360 km (224 miles) with full warload
Load: Three 23 mm cannon, plus up to 500 kg (1,102 lb) of bombs or unguided rockets

MiG-15UTI 'Midget' was a two-seat trainer

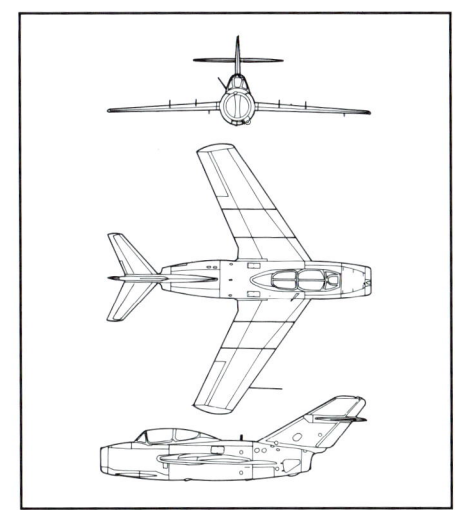

MiG-15UTI 'Midget'

NORTH AMERICAN F-86 SABRE (U.S.A.)

F-86F Sabre

The Sabre was the most important American air combat fighter in the Korean War. In 1944 the U.S. Army Air Forces contracted for three XP-86 prototypes for a day fighter that could also double in the escort and ground-attack roles. When the fruits of German aerodynamic research became available to the Americans after World War II, the type was reworked to incorporate swept flying surfaces, and the first such prototype flew in October 1947 with a 1701-kg (3,750-lb) thrust General Electric TG-180 (later J35-GE-3) axial-flow turbojet. The type was then re-engined with the General Electric J47 turbojet to become the YP-86A, leading to the P-86A (later F-86A) production model with the 2200-kg (4,850-lb) thrust J47-GE-1 engine.

These 554 aircraft with four J47 marks up to a thrust of 2359-kg (5,200-lb) were followed in chronological order by the 456 F-86Es with a slab tailplane and the 3877-kg (5,200-lb) thrust J47-GE-27, the 2,540 F-86Fs with the 2708-kg (5,970-lb) thrust J47-GE-27 and, in later aircraft, the '6-3' wing with extended leading edges, the 2,504 F-86D redesigned night and all-weather fighters with the 2517-kg (5,550-lb) thrust J47-GE-33, the 473 F-86H fighter-bombers with the 4037-kg (8,900-lb) thrust J73-GE-3, greater span and a deeper fuselage, the 341 examples of the F-86K simplified version of the F-86D with the 2461-kg (5,425-lb) J47-GE-17B, and the 981 examples of the F-86L rebuilt version of the F-86D with a larger wing and updated electronics. The Sabre was also built in Australia as the CAC Sabre in Mk 30, 31 and 32 versions with two 30-mm cannon and the Rolls-Royce Avon turbojet, and in Canada as the Canadair Sabre in Mk 2, 4 and 6 versions with the Orenda turbojet.

North American F-86E Sabre

NORTH AMERICAN F-86F SABRE
Role: Day fighter
Crew/Accommodation: One
Power Plant: One 2,708 kgp (5,970 lb s.t.) General Electric J47-GE-27 turbojet
Dimensions: Span 11.3 m (37.08 ft); length 11.43 m (37.5 ft); wing area 26.76 m² (288 sq ft)
Weights: Empty 4,967 kg (10,950 lb); MTOW 7,711 kg (17,000 lb)
Performance: Maximum speed 1,110 km/h (690 mph) at sea level; operational ceiling 15,240 m (50,000 ft); range 1,263 km (785 miles) without external fuel
Load: Six .5 inch machine guns, plus up to 907 kg (2,000 lb) of bombs or fuel carried externally

F-86F Sabre

JET FIGHTERS

SAAB 29 (Sweden)

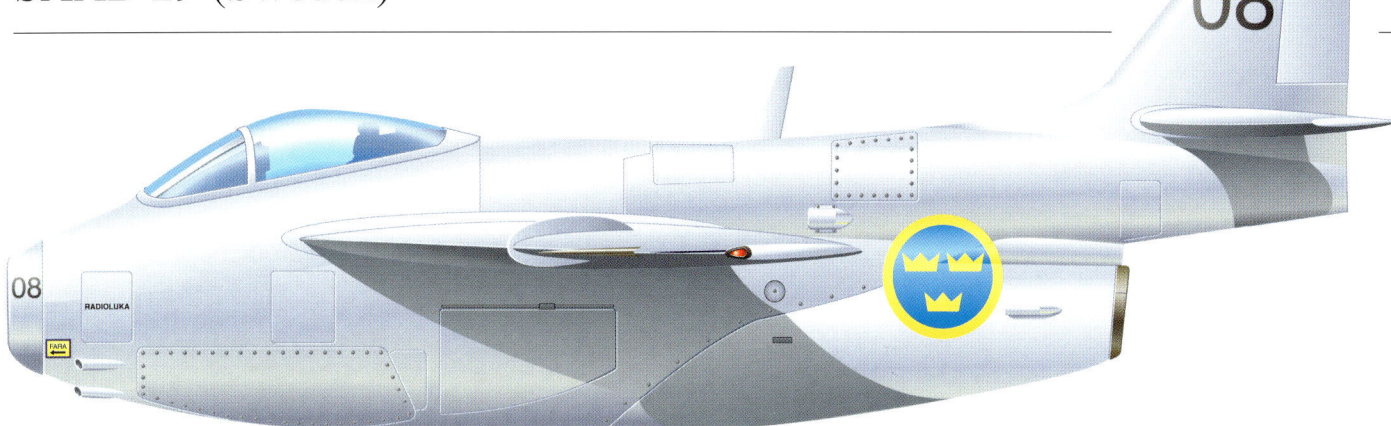

In 1943 SAAB flew its first fighter, the SAAB 21, an unconventional twin-boom pusher type with an ejection seat for the pilot. In 1947 a jet version was first flown as the SAAB 21R, with a British de Havilland Goblin turbojet replacing the earlier piston engine. Although the jet version was put into production and then operated in fighter and attack versions from 1949 to 1955, SAAB by then had much more advanced projects in hand, of which the SAAB 29 became the company's next production jet fighter and, historically, the first European swept-wing fighter to enter operational service.

The Goblin jet engine, then in production in Sweden, also powered Vampire fighters bought direct from Britain to boost Swedish squadrons, and it was logical therefore to design the SAAB 29 around the Goblin. However, with the appearance of the more-powerful 2,268 kg (5,000 lb thrust) de Havilland Ghost engine, the SAAB 29 was revised to use this (as the RM2).

Initial design work on the SAAB 29 had begun as early as 1945, then known as project R 1001. As a completely new design, SAAB chose a 'straight through' fuselage layout, with a nose air intake to feed the jet engine, the latter which exhausted below the narrowing boom-like rear portion of the fuselage and a conventional tail. However, by far the most important design feature was the eventual adoption of wings with 25 degrees of sweepback, original plans to use straight wings having been reviewed after a SAAB engineer had shown foresight to act upon confiscated wartime German technical research material on advanced wing shapes seen during a visit to Switzerland.

The adoption of swept wings followed considerable wind-tunnel testing plus actual flight testing using scaled wings fitted to a Safir lightplane known for research purposes as the SAAB 201.

Featuring also a pressurised cockpit, the first of four prototype SAAB 29s first flew on 1 September 1948 and proved capable of bettering its designed maximum speed of 1,050 km/h (650 mph). Production J 29As were delivered from May 1951, initially to F13 day fighter Wing at Norrköping. Because of its stubby appearance, the fighter gained the nickname Tunnan (Barrel).

After the J 29A came the longer-range SAAB 29B of 1953 appearance, used both as the J 29B fighter and A 29B attack aircraft. The S 29C was a photo reconnaissance variant, which in 1955 established a world closed-circuit speed record of 906 km/h (563 mph). A few J 29Ds followed with Swedish-built afterburners, while the J 29E introduced the 'dog-tooth' wing leading edge to raise the critial Mach number and offer improvements in transonic handling. The final version was the J 29F, with dog-tooth wings, an afterburner to the Ghost 50 (RM2B) engine that raised thrust to 2,800 kg (6,170 lb), and the ability to carry two Sidewinder air-to-air missiles. In total, the Flygvapnet received 661 SAAB 29s, and many Bs were subsequently upgraded to F standard, while Cs later received dog-tooth wings. Austria took in thirty ex-Swedish J 29Fs from 1961. The final flight of a Tunnan was recorded in 1976.

Two SAAB J 29F in flight

SAAB J 29F 'Tunnan'
Role: Fighter and attack
Crew/Accommodation: Pilot
Power Plant: One 2,800 kgp (6,170 lb s.t.) SFA-built RM2B turbojet with reheat (de Havilland Ghost 50)
Dimensions: Span 11.0 m (36.09 ft); length 10.23m (33.56 ft); wing area 24 m^2 (258 sq ft)
Weights: MTOW typically 8,000 kg (17,637 lb), but 8,375 kg (18,464 lb) possible
Performance: Maximum speed 1,060 km/h (658 mph); operational ceiling 15,500 m (50,850 ft); range 1,100 km (683 miles)
Load: Four 20 mm cannon plus rockets or two Sidewinder missiles

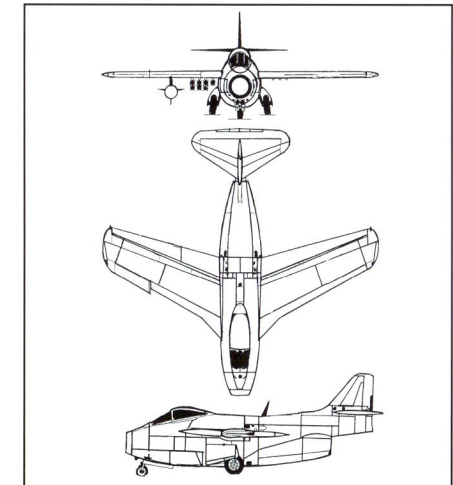

SAAB J 29F

HAWKER HUNTER (United Kingdom)

Hunter FGA.Mk 58

The Hunter was numerically the most successful of British post-World War II fighters, with 1,972 built including 445 manufactured under licence in Belgium and the Netherlands. The type still serves in modest numbers with a few air forces, though not as a fighter. This superb fighter resulted from a British need to replace the obsolescent Gloster Meteor with a more advanced type offering transonic performance and the P.1067 prototype first flew in July 1951, and was followed just one month later by the first Hunter F.Mk 1 pre-production aircraft.

The first production article flew in May 1953, and the Hunter F.Mk 1 entered squadron service in July 1954. These aircraft were powered by the Rolls-Royce Avon turbojet, but the Hunter F.Mk 2 used the Armstrong Siddeley Sapphire Mk 101 turbojet. Further evolution led to the similar Hunter F.Mks 4 and 5 with more fuel and underwing armament capability, the former with the Avon Mk 115/121 and the latter with the Sapphire Mk 101. The Hunter F.Mk 6 introduced the Avon Mk 200 series turbojet in its Mk 203/207 forms, greater fuel capacity, along with the underwing armament of the F.Mk 4. The F.Mk 6 was later developed as the Hunter FGA.Mk 9 definitive ground-attack fighter with the dogtoothed leading edges and Avon Mk 207 engine.

There were also tactical reconnaissance variants based on the FGA.Mk 9 and produced in Hunter FR.Mk 10 and FR.Mk 11 forms for the RAF and Fleet Air Arm respectively. Another variant was the side-by-side two-seat trainer, pioneered in the P.1101 prototype that first flew in mid-1955. This was produced in Hunter T.Mks 7 and 8 forms for the RAF and Fleet Air Arm respectively. Export derivatives of the single- and two-seaters were numerous, and Switzerland continued to acquire large numbers of refurbished Hunters for roles including ground attack.

A Hawker Hunter F.Mk 1 used as an instructional airframe

HAWKER HUNTER F.Mk 6
Role: Day fighter
Crew/Accommodation: One
Power Plant: One 4,605 kgp (10,150 lb s.t.) Rolls-Royce Avon Mk 207 turbojet
Dimensions: Span 10.25 m (33.33 ft); length 13.97 m (45.83 ft); wing area 32.42 m² (349 sq ft)
Weights: Empty 6,505 kg (14,22 lb); MTOW 8,051 kg (17,750 lb)
Performance: Maximum speed 1,002 km/h (623 mph) at 10,975 m (36,000 ft); operational ceiling 14,630 m (48,000 ft); range 789 km (490 miles) on internal fuel only
Load: Four 30 mm cannon

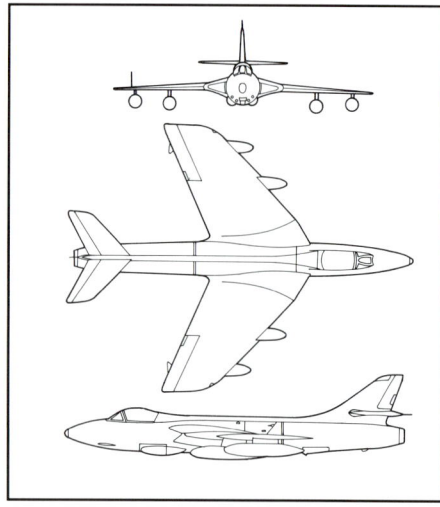

Hawker Hunter FGA.Mk 9

JET FIGHTERS

DASSAULT MYSTERE and SUPER MYSTERE (France)

Mystère IVA

At the end of World War II, Marcel Bloch was released from a German concentration camp, promptly changed his named to Dassault and started to rebuild his original aircraft company as Avions Marcel Dassault, the premier French manufacturer of warplanes. After gaining experience in the design and construction of jet-powered fighters with the straight-winged M.D. 450 Ouragan fighter-bomber, Dassault turned his attention to a swept-wing design, the Mystère (Mystery). This first flew in the form of the M.D. 452 Mystère I prototype form during February 1951, and was followed by eight more prototypes each with the Rolls-Royce Tay turbojet: two more Mystère Is, two Mystère IIAs and four Mystère IIBs. Then came 11 pre-production Mystère IICs with the 3000-kg (6,614-lb) thrust SNECMA Atar 101 turbojet, and these paved the way for the Mystère IV production prototype that first flew in September 1952 with the Tay turbojet but thinner and more highly swept wings, a longer oval-section fuselage, and modified tail surfaces. There followed nine Mystère IVA pre-production aircraft and finally more than 480 production fighters, of which the first 50 retained the Tay but the others used the 3500-kg (7,716-lb) thrust Hispano-Suiza Verdun 350 turbojet.

Further development led to the Mystère IVB prototype with a Rolls-Royce Avon turbojet, a thinner and more highly swept wing, and a revised fuselage of lower drag. The resulting Super Mystère B1 production prototype flew in March 1955 with an afterburning turbojet as the first genuinely supersonic aircraft of European design, and was followed by 185 examples of the Super Mystère B2 production model with the 4460-kg (9,833-lb) thrust Atar 101G-2/3 afterburning turbojet. Some aircraft were supplied to Israel, which modified a number with the 4218-kg (9,300-lb) thrust Pratt & Whitney J52-P-8A non-afterburning turbojet.

Dassault Mystère IVA fighters of the French Air Force's EC 8 wing

DASSAULT MYSTERE IVA
Role: Strike fighter
Crew/Accommodation: One
Power Plant: One 3,500 kgp (7,716 lb s.t.) Hispano-Suiza Verdun 350 turbojet
Dimensions: Span 11.13 m (36.5 ft); length 12.83 m (42.1 ft); wing area 32 m² (344.5 sq ft)
Weights: Empty 5,875 kg (12,950 lb); MTOW 9,096 kg (20,050 lb)
Performance: Maximum speed 1,120 km/h (604 knots) at sea level; operational ceiling 13,716 m (45,000 ft); range 460 km (248 naut. miles)
Load: Two 30 mm DEFA cannon, plus to up 907 kg (2,000 lb) of externally carried bombs

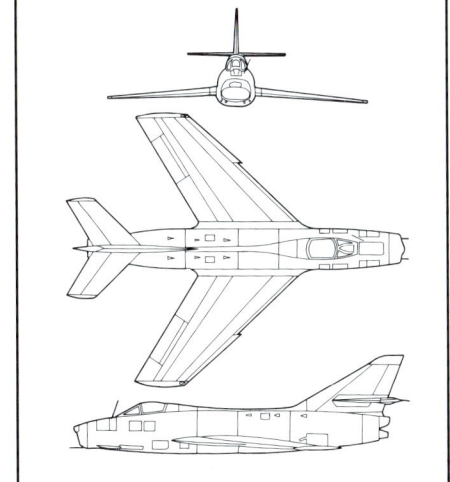

Dassault Super Mystère B2

19

CONVAIR F-102 DELTA DAGGER and F-106 DELTA DART (U.S.A.)

F-106A Delta Dart

These two delta-winged fighters were designed specifically for air defence of the continental United States and were among the first aircraft in the world designed as part of a complete weapon system integrating airframe, sensors, and weapons. The YF-102 was developed on the basis of data derived from the experimental programme undertaken with the XF-92A, which itself was derived from American assessment of German research into delta-winged aircraft during World War II. The Model 8 was planned to provide the U.S. Air Force with an 'Ultimate Interceptor' for the defence of North American airspace, and was intended to possess Mach 2+ performance and carry the very advanced MX-1179 Electronic Control System. The resulting Model 8-80 was ordered as a single YF-102 prototype and first flew in October 1952 with a 4400-kg (9,700-lb) thrust Pratt & Whitney J57-P-11 turbojet. This prototype was soon lost in an accident but had already displayed disappointing performance.

The airframe of the succeeding YF-102A was redesigned with Whitcomb area ruling to reduce drag, and this improved performance to a degree that made feasible the introduction of F-102A single-seat fighter and TF-102A two-seat trainer variants. The MX-1179 ECS had proved too difficult for the technology of the time, so the less advanced MG-3 fire-control system was adopted for these models, of which 875 and 111 respectively were built.

Greater effort went into the development of the true Mach 2 version, which was developed as the F-102B but then ordered as the F-106 before the first of two YF-106A prototypes flew in December 1956. The F-106A single-seat fighter and F-102B two-seat trainer versions were produced to the extent of 277 and 63 aircraft respectively, and these served into the later 1980s.

Convair F-106A Delta Dart

CONVAIR-F-106A DELTA DART
Role: All-weather interceptor
Crew/Accommodation: One
Power Plant: One 11,115 kgp (24,500 lb s.t.) Pratt & Whitney J75-P-17 turbojet with reheat
Dimensions: Span 11.67 m (38.29 ft); length 21.56 m (70.73 ft); wing area 64.83 m² (697.8 sq ft)
Weights: Empty 10,904 kg (24,038 lb); MTOW 17,779 kg (39,195 lb)
Performance: Maximum speed 2,135 km/h (1,152 knots) at 10,668 m (35,000 ft); operational ceiling 16,063 m (52,700 ft); radius 789 km (490 miles) on internal fuel only
Load: One 20 mm multi-barrel cannon, plus one long-range and four medium-range air-to-air missiles

A Convair F-106A Delta Dart

JET FIGHTERS

VOUGHT F-8 CRUSADER (U.S.A.)

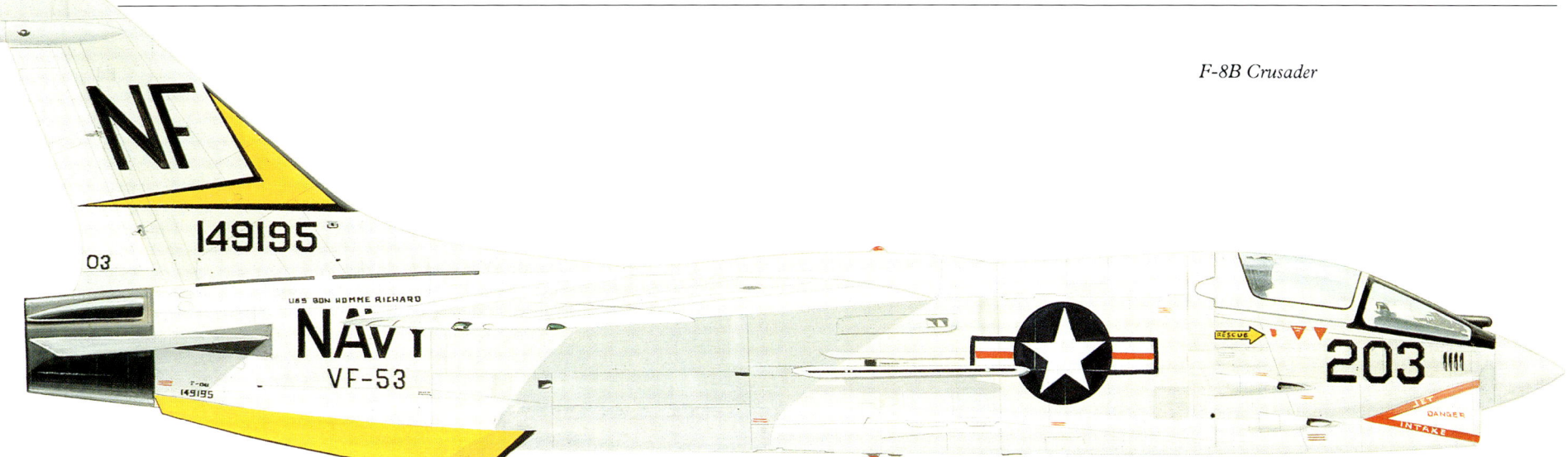

F-8B Crusader

A slightly later contemporary of the North American F-100 Super Sabre that used practically the same powerplant, the Crusader carrierborne fighter was an altogether more capable machine despite the additional fixed weight of its naval equipment. The design's most interesting feature was a variable-incidence wing that allowed the fuselage to be kept level during take-off and landing, thereby improving the pilot's fields of vision. The type resulted from a 1952 U.S. Navy requirement for an air-superiority fighter with truly supersonic performance, and from eight submissions the Vought design was selected in May 1953.

The first of two XF8U-1 prototypes flew in March 1955 with the 6713-kg (14,800-lb) thrust Pratt & Whitney J57-P-11 turbojet. Deliveries to operational squadrons began in March 1957 of the F8U-1 with the 7348-kg (16,200-lb) thrust J57-P-4A, four 20-mm cannon, rockets in an underfuselage pack and, as a retrofit, Sidewinder air-to air missiles. Production totalled 318, and from 1962 these aircraft were redesignated F-8A. There followed 30 examples of the F8U-1E (F-8B) with limited all-weather capability, 187 examples of the F8U-2 (F-8C) with the 7666-kg (16,900-lb) thrust J57-P-16, 152 examples of the F8U-2N (F-8D) with the 8,165-kg (18,000-lb) thrust J57-P-20, extra fuel and four Sidewinder missiles, and 286 examples of the F8U-2NE (F-8E) with the 8165-kg (18,000-lb) thrust J57-P-20A, advanced radar and provision for 1,814 kg (4,000 lb) of external stores on four underwing hardpoints. In addition, 42 F-8E (FN)s were built for the French Navy, the only remaining type in service, to be replaced by Rafales. The F-8H to L were rebuilds of older aircraft to an improved standard with a strengthened airframe and blown flaps, and a reconnaissance variant was the F8U-1P (RF-8A); 73 were later rebuilt to RF-8G standard with the J57-P-20A.

VOUGHT F-8E CRUSADER
Role: Naval carrierborne fighter
Crew/Accommodation: One
Power Plant: One 8,165 kgp (18,000 lb s.t.) Pratt & Whitney J57-P-20 turbojet with reheat
Dimensions: Span 10.9 m (35.7 ft); length 16.5 m (54.2 ft); wing area 34.8 m² (375 sq ft)
Weights: Empty 8,960 kg (19,750 lb); MTOW 15,420 kg (34,000 lb)
Performance: Maximum speed 1,802 km/h (973 knots) Mach 1.7 at 12,192 m (40,000 ft); operational ceiling 17,374 m (57,000 ft); radius 966 km (521 naut. miles)
Load: Four 30 mm cannon, plus up to 2,268 kg (5,000 lb) of externally carried weapons, which can include four short-range air-to-air missiles

The French Navy's version of the Vought Crusader is the F-8E(FN)

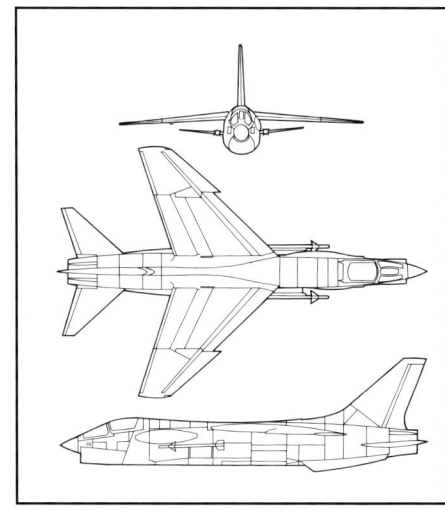

Vought F8U-2 Crusader

SUD-OUEST S.O.4050 VAUTOUR (France)

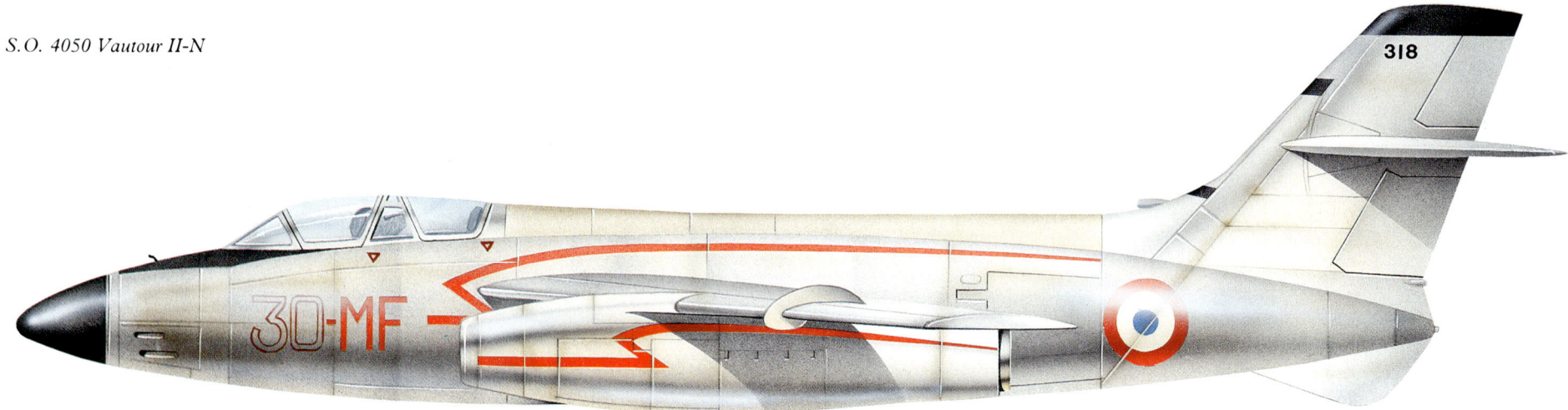

S.O. 4050 Vautour II-N

In the late 1940s, Sud-Ouest produced two half-scale research aircraft as the S.O.M.1 air-launched research glider and its powered version, the S.O.M.2 with a Rolls-Royce Derwent turbojet. The company then evolved the S.O.4000 full-scale prototype with two Rolls-Royce Nene turbojets (licence-built by Hispano-Suiza) in the rear fuselage and the unusual landing gear of a single nosewheel and four main wheels, the latter arranged in tandem pairs.

The S.O.4000 first flew in March 1951, and paved the way for the S.O.4050 Vautour (Vulture) prototype with swept flying surfaces and a landing gear arrangement comprising two-twin wheel main units in tandem under the fuselage and single-wheel outriggers under the nacelles of the wing-mounted engines. The first of three prototypes was a two-seat night fighter and flew in October 1952 with 2400-kg (5,291-lb) thrust SNECMA Atar 101B turbojets; the second machine was a single-seat ground-attack type with 2820-kg (6,217-lb) thrust Atar 101Ds; and the third machine was a two-seat bomber with Armstrong Siddeley Sapphire turbojets. There followed six pre-production aircraft before it was decided to procure all three variants with a powerplant standardized as two 3500-kg (7,716-lb) thrust Atar 101Es. Even so, production totalled just 140 aircraft. These comprised 30 single-seat Vautour II-A ground-attack aircraft, 40 two-seat Vautour II-B bombers, and 70 two-seat Vautour II-N night fighters, with equipment and armament optimized for the three types' specific role. The first of these three types flew in April 1956, July 1957 and October 1956 respectively. Some 18 aircraft were later supplied to Israel, and after retrofit with slab tailplanes, the Vautour II-N became the Vautour II-1N.

SUD S.O. 4050 VAUTOUR II-N
Role: All-weather/night fighter
Crew/Accommodation: Two
Power Plant: Two 3,300 kgp (7,275 lb s.t.) SNECMA Atar 101E-3 turbojets
Dimensions: Span 15.1 m (49.54 ft); length 16.5 m (54.13 ft); wing area 45.3 m² (487.6 sq ft)
Weights: Empty 9,880 kg (21,782 lb); MTOW 17,000 kg (37,479 lb)
Performance: Maximum speed 958 km/h (595 mph) at 12,200 m (40,026 ft); operational ceiling 14,000 m (45, 932 ft); range 2,750 km (1,709 miles) with maximum fuel
Load: Four 20 mm cannon

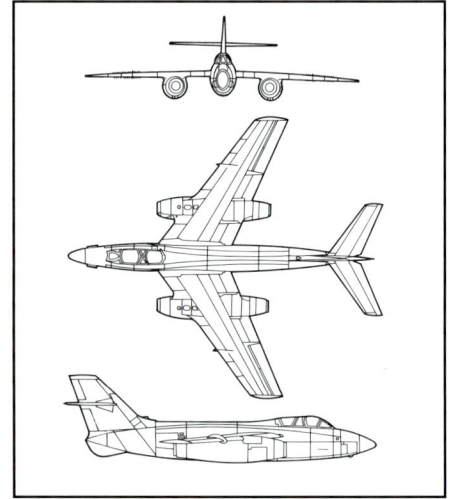

Sud-Ouest S.O.4050 Vautour II

Sud-Ouest S.O.4050 Vautour

JET FIGHTERS

LOCKHEED F-104 STARFIGHTER (U.S.A.)

F-104S Super Starfighter

The Starfighter resulted from the U.S. Air Force's experiences in the Korean War, where the need for a fast-climbing interceptor became clear. The type was planned by 'Kelly' Johnson with the smallest airframe that would accommodate the most powerful available axial-flow turbojet. This resulted in a fighter possessing a long and basically cylindrical fuselage with unswept and diminutive wings, plus a large T-tail assembly.

The first of two XF-104 prototypes first flew in March 1954 with an interim engine, the 4627-kg (10,200-lb) thrust Wright XJ65-W-6, and four years of troubled development followed with 17 YF-104As before the F-104A entered service with a longer fuselage accommodating the 6713-kg (14,800-lb) thrust J79-GE-3 engine, and an armament of one 20-mm multi-barrel cannon and two AIM-9 Sidewinder air-to-air missiles. The USAF eventually ordered only 296 examples of the Starfighter in variants that included 153 F-104A interceptors, 26 F-104B tandem-seat trainers, 77 F-104C tactical strike fighters with provision for a 907-kg (2,000-lb) external load, and 21 F-104D tandem-seat trainers. The commercial success of the type was then ensured by the adoption of the much-improved F-104G all-weather multi-role type by a NATO consortium. This model had a strengthened airframe, a larger vertical tail, greater power, and more advanced electronics, and itself spawned the F-104J interceptor that was built in Japan. This multi-national programme resulted in the largely licensed production of another 1,986 aircraft up to 1983. The F-104G itself produced TF-104 trainer and RF-104 reconnaissance variants, and Italy developed the special F-104S variant as a dedicated interceptor with better radar and medium-range Sparrow and Aspide air-to-air missiles.

Lockheed F-104G Starfighters of European air forces

LOCKHEED F-104A STARFIGHTER
Role: Interceptor
Crew/Accommodation: One
Power Plant: One 6,713 kgp (14,800 lb s.t.) General Electric J79-GE-3B turbojet with reheat
Dimensions: Span 6.63 m (21.75 ft); length 16.66 m (54.66 ft); wing area 18.2 m² (196.1 sq ft)
Weights: Empty 6,071 kg (13,384 lb); MTOW 11,271 kg (25,840 lb)
Performance: Maximum speed 1,669 km/h (1,037 mph) at 15,240 m (50,000 ft) operational ceiling 19,750 m (64,795 ft); range 1,175 km (730 miles) with full warload
Load: One 20 mm multi-barrel cannon and two short-range air-to-air missiles

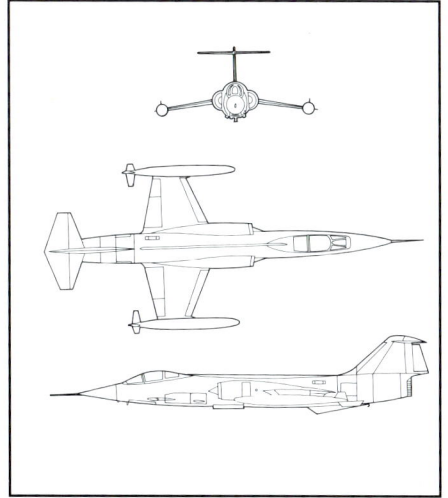

Lockheed F-104G Starfighter

REPUBLIC F-105 THUNDERCHIEF (U.S.A.)

F-105 D Thunderchief

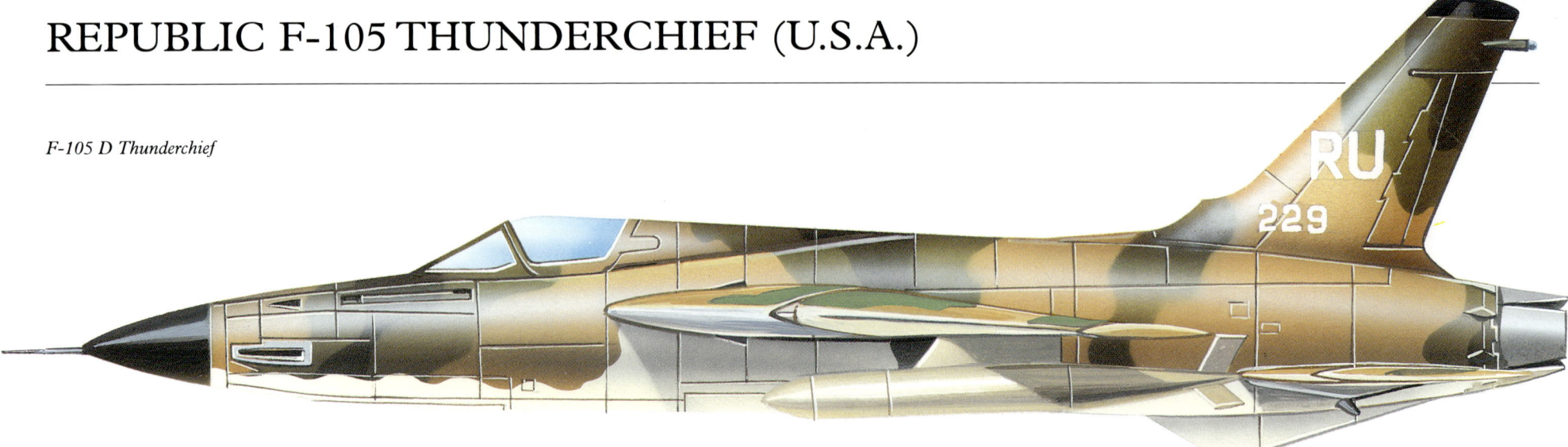

The Thunderchief was the final major type to come from the Republic company before its merger into the Fairchild organization, and accorded well with its manufacturer's reputation for massive tactical warplanes. The type was schemed as a successor to the F-84F Thunderstreak and was therefore a strike fighter, but one that offered the advantages of an internal weapons bay able to accommodate 3629-kg (8,000-lb) of stores and fully supersonic performance. This last was provided by the use of a powerful afterburning turbojet in an advanced airframe incorporating the lessons of the area-rule principle.

Two YF-105A prototypes were ordered, and the first of these flew in October 1956 with the 6804-kg (15,000-lb) thrust Pratt & Whitney J57-P-25 turbojet and an 'unwaisted' fuselage. No production followed, for the availability of the new J75 engine and the area-rule theory resulted first in another four prototypes designated YF-105B and powered by 7471-kg (16,470-lb) thrust J75-P-3. Production thus began with 71 F-105B aircraft modelled on the YF-105B and its area-ruled 'waisted' fuselage and forward-swept inlets in the wing roots for the 7802-kg (17,200-lb) thrust J75-P-5 engine. The major variant was the F-105D, of which 610 were built with all-weather avionics, an improved nav/attack system, the 7802-kg (17,200-lb) J75-P-19W turbojet and provision for up to 6350-kg (14,000-lb) of ordnance carried on four underwing hardpoints as well as in the internal load.

The final version was the F-105F tandem two-seat conversion trainer, and of 86 aircraft 60 were later converted to EF-105F (and then F-105G) 'Wild Weasel' defence-suppression aircraft. These were fitted with special radar-detection equipment and anti-radar missiles, and played an important part in American air operations over North Vietnam.

REPUBLIC F-105D THUNDERCHIEF
Role: Fighter
Crew/Accommodation: One
Power Plant: One 11,113 kgp (24,500 lb s.t.) Pratt & Whitney J75-P-15W turbojet with reheat
Dimensions: Span 10.65 m (34.94 ft); length 19.58 m (64.25 ft); wing area 35.76 m² (385 sq ft)
Weights: Empty 12,474 kg (27,500 lb); MTOW 23,834 kg (52,546 lb)
Performance: Maximum speed 2,369 km/h (1,279 knots) Mach 2.23 at 11,000 m (36,090 ft); operational ceiling 12,802 m (42,000 ft); radius 1,152 km (662 naut. miles)
Load: One 20 mm multi-barrel cannon, plus up to 6,350 kg (14,000 lb) of weapons/fuel

Republic F-105G Thunderchief

Republic F-105D single-seaters and, in the foreground, an F-105F two-seater

MILITARY AIRCRAFT
SAAB 35 DRAKEN (Sweden)

JET FIGHTERS

F35 Draken

An even more remarkable achievement than the Saab 32, the Saab 35 Draken (Dragon) was designed as an interceptor of transonic bombers. This role demanded supersonic speed, a very high rate of climb, better than average range and endurance, and a sizeable weapon load. The tactical philosophy of the Swedish Air Force also dictated that the new type should have STOL capability so that it could operate from lengths of straight road during dispersed operations. The fighter was therefore designed on the basis of a slender circular-section fuselage and a double-delta wing in a combination that provided large lifting area and fuel capacity at minimum profile drag. To achieve much the same performance as the slightly later English Electric Lightning powered by two Rolls-Royce Avon afterburning turbojets, the design team opted for such a single example of the same engine built under licence in Sweden as the Flygmotor RM6. The layout was evaluated successfully in the Saab 210 research aircraft that was in essence a scaled-down Saab 35 and first flew in February 1952 with the 476-kg (1,050-lb) thrust Armstrong Siddeley Adder turbojet.

The first prototype of the Saab 35 flew in October 1955, and the J 35A initial production variant began to enter service in 1958. Production totalled 525 in variants such as the J 35A fighter with the 7000-kg (14,432-lb) thrust RM6B, the J 35B improved fighter with collision-course radar and a data-link system, the Sk 35C tandem-seat operational trainer, the J 35D fighter with the 7830-kg (17,262-lb) thrust RM6C and more advanced electronics, the S 35E tactical reconnaissance aircraft and the J 35F with more advanced radar and Hughes Falcon air-to-air missiles. The type was also exported as the Saab 35X, and surviving J 35Fs have been upgraded to J 35J standard for service into the 1990s.

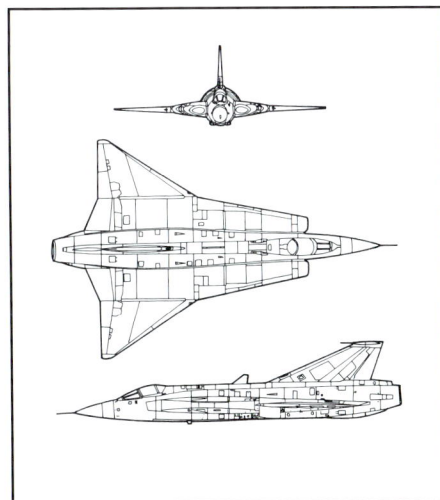

Saab 35 Draken

SAAB 35/J 35 DRAKEN
Role: Interceptor/strike/reconnaissance
Crew/Accommodation: One
Power Plant: One 7,830 kgp (17,262 lb s.t.) Flygmotor-built Rolls-Royce Avon RM6C turbojet with reheat
Dimensions: Span 9.4 m (30.83 ft); length 15.4 m (50.33 ft); wing area 50 m² (538 sq ft)
Weights: Empty (not available); MTOW 16,000 kg (35,274 lb)
Performance: Maximum/Cruise speed 2,150 km/h (1,160 mph) Mach 2.023 at 11,000 m (36,090 ft); operational ceiling 18,300 m (60,039 ft); range 1,149 km (620 naut. miles) with 2,000 lb warload
Load: Two 30 mm cannon, plus up to 4,082 kg (9,000 lb) of bombs

The J 35F was the definitive interceptor of the Saab Draken family

25

DASSAULT MIRAGE III and IAI KFIR (France and Israel)

IAI Kfir C-7

The Mirage was designed to meet a 1954 French requirement for a small all-weather supersonic interceptor, and emerged as the delta-winged M.D.550 Mirage prototype for a first flight in June 1955 with two 980-kg (2,160-lb) thrust Armstrong Siddeley Viper turbojets. The type was too small for any realistic military use, and a slightly larger Mirage II was planned; this was not built, both these initial concepts being abandoned in favour of the still larger Mirage III that first flew in November 1956 with an Atar 101G-1 afterburning turbojet. Further development led to the Mirage IIIA pre-production type with an Atar 9B of 6,000-kg (13,228-lb) afterburning thrust boosting speed from Mach 1.65 to 2.2 at altitude.

The type went into widespread production for the French forces and for export, and as such was a considerable commercial success for Dassault, especially after Israeli success with the type in the 1967 'Six-Day War'. The basic variants became the Mirage IIIB two-seat trainer, the Mirage IIIC single-seat interceptor, the Mirage IIIE single-seat strike fighter and the Mirage IIIR reconnaissance aircraft. The Mirage 5 was produced as a clear-weather type, though the miniaturization of electronics in the 1970s and 1980s have allowed the installation or retrofit of avionics that make most Mirage 5 and up-engined Mirage 50 models superior to the baseline Mirage III models. Israel produced a Mirage 5 variant as the IAI Kfir with a General Electric J79 afterburning turbojet and advanced electronics, and this spawned the impressive Kfir-C2 and later variants with canard foreplanes for much improved field and combat performance. Many surviving Mirages have been modernized to incorporate aerodynamics, avionics and weapon improvements, with newly-named variants including the Chilian ENAER Pantera, Belgian SABCA Elkan (for Chile), and South African Denel Cheetah.

Dassault Mirage 5

DASSAULT MIRAGE IIIE
Role: Strike fighter
Crew/Accommodation: One
Power Plant: One 6,200 kgp (13,670 lb s.t.) SNECMA Atar 9C turbojet, plus provision for one 1,500 kgp (3,307 lb s.t.) SEPR 844 rocket engine
Dimensions: Span 8.22 m (27 ft); length 15.03 m (49.26 ft); wing area 34.85 m² (375 sq ft)
Weights: Empty 7,050 kg (15,540 lb); MTOW 13,000 kg (29,760 lb)
Performance: Maximum speed 2,350 km/h (1,268 knots) Mach 2.21 at 12,000 m (39,375 ft); operational ceiling 17,000 m (55,775 ft); radius 1,200 km (648 naut. miles)
Load: Two 30 mm DEFA cannon, plus up to 1,362 kg (3,000 lb) of externally carried ordnance

A Dassault-Breguet Mirage IIING

MIKOYAN MiG-21 'FISHBED' (U.S.S.R.)

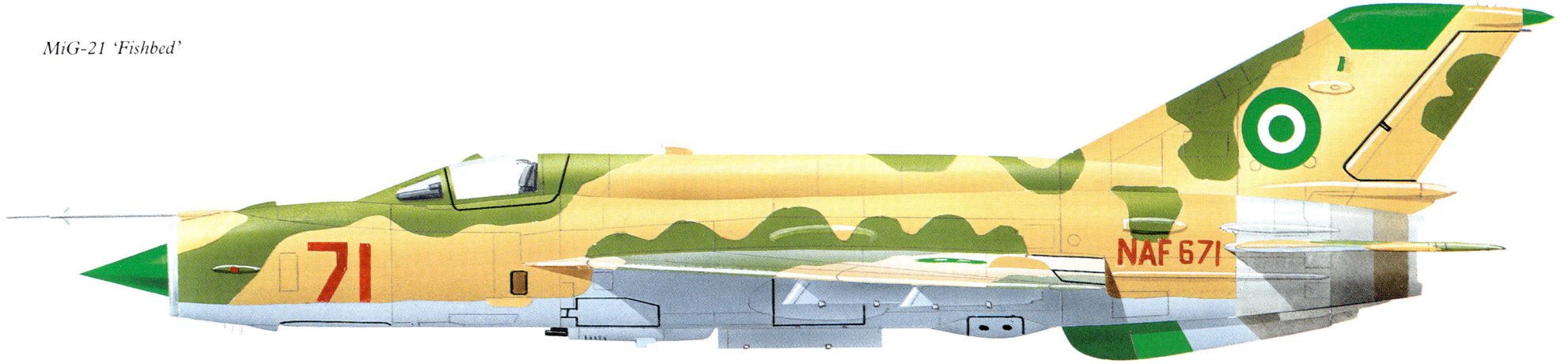

MiG-21 'Fishbed'

The MiG-21 (NATO name 'Fishbed') was designed, after the U.S.S.R. had digested the implications of the Korean War, to provide a short-range interceptor. The type was analogous to the Lockheed F-104 Starfighter in rationale, but was a radically different aircraft based on a tailed delta configuration, small overall size, and light weight to ensure adequate performance on just one relatively low-powered afterburning turbojet, the Tumansky R-11, that was only slightly larger and heavier than the RD-9 used in the preceding MiG-19's twin-engined powerplant.

Differently configured Ye-2A and Ye-5 prototypes were flown in 1956, the latter paving the way for the definitive Ye-6 prototype that flew in May 1958. 10,158 MiG-21s were built in the U.S.S.R. (others in India, China as the J-7, and Czechoslovakia) in variants such as the MiG-21 clear-weather interceptor, MiG 21PF limited all-weather fighter with search and track radar, MiG-21 PFS fighter with blown flaps and provision for RATO units, MiG-21FL export version of the MiG-21PFS but without blown flaps or RATO provision, MiG-21PFM improved version of the MiG-21PFS, MiG-21S/SM second-generation dual-role fighter with a larger dorsal hump and four rather than two underwing hardpoints, MiG-21M export version of the MiG-21S, MiG-21R tactical reconnaissance version, MiG-21MF with the more powerful but lighter R-13-30 engine, MiG-21RF reconnaissance version of the MiG-21MF, MiG-21SMT aerodynamically refined version of the MiG-21MF with increased fuel and ECM capability and MiG-21bis third generation multi-role fighter. There have also been three MiG-21U 'Mongol' conversion trainer variants. Currently, upgrades are offered by Russia and others, including the MiG-21-93 as chosen by India.

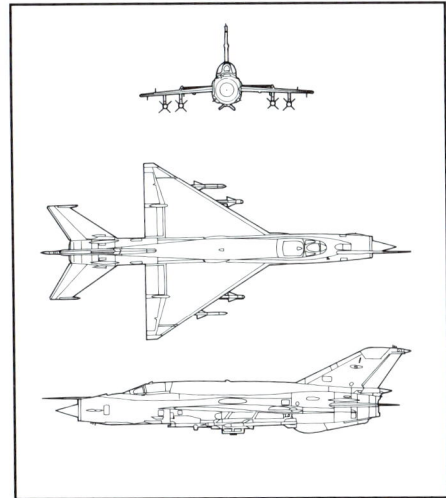

MiG-21 'Fishbed-K'

MIKOYAN-GUREVICH MiG-21SMT 'FISHBED-K'
Role: Strike fighter
Crew/Accommodation: One
Power Plant: One 6,600 kgp (14,550 lb s.t) Tumansky R-13 turbojet with reheat
Dimensions: Span 7.15 m (23.46 ft); length 13.46 m (44.16 ft); wing area 23 m² (247.57 sq ft)
Weights: Empty 5,450 kg (12,015 lb); MTOW 7,750 kg (17,085 lb)
Performance: Maximum speed 2,230 km/h (1,386 mph) Mach 2.1 at 12,000 m (39,370 ft); operational ceiling 18,000 m (59,055 ft); radius 500 km (311 miles) with full warload
Load: Two 23 mm cannon, plus up to 1,000 kg (2,205 lb) of air-to-air missiles or bombs depending upon mission

The Mikoyan-Gurevich MiG-21

ENGLISH ELECTRIC LIGHTNING (United Kingdom)

Lightning F.Mk 6

The Lightning was the United Kingdom's first supersonic fighter. The type offered superlative speed and climb performance, but was always limited by poor range and indifferent armament. The origins of the type lay in the P.1A, which resulted from a 1947 requirement for a supersonic research aircraft. The first of three prototypes flew in August 1954 and later revealed supersonic performance on two Bristol Siddeley non-afterburning turbojets. It was seen that the type had the makings of an interceptor, and the type was revised as the P.1B that first flew in April 1957 with two superimposed Rolls-Royce Avon turbojets. After a lengthy development with 20 pre-production aircraft, the type began to enter service in 1960 as the Lightning F.Mk 1 with two 30-mm cannon and two Firestreak air-to-air missiles.

Later variants were the Lightning F.Mk 1A with inflight-refuelling capability, the Lightning F.Mk 2 with improved electronics and fully variable afterburners, the Lightning F.Mk 3 with 7420-kg (16,360-lb) thrust Avon Mk 300 series engines, provision for overwing drop tanks, a square-topped vertical tail, improved radar, no guns, and a pair of Red Top air-to-air missiles that offered all-aspect engagement capability in place of the earlier marks' pursuit-course Firestreak missiles.

The final variant was the Lightning F.Mk 6 (originally lightning F.Mk 3A) with a revised wing with cambered and kinked leading edges, and a ventral tank that virtually doubled fuel capacity while also accommodating a pair of 30-mm cannon. There were also two side-by-side trainer models, the Lightning T.Mks 4 and 5; these were based on the F.Mk 1A and F.Mk 3 respectively, and retained full combat capability. For export there was the Lighting Mk 50 series of fighters and trainers.

ENGLISH ELECTRIC/BAC LIGHTNING F.Mk 6
Role: Interceptor fighter
Crew/Accommodation: One
Power Plant: Two 7,420 kgp (16,360 lb s.t.) Rolls-Royce Avon 300 turbojets with reheat
Dimensions: Span 10.61 m (34.9 ft); length 16.84 m (55.25 ft); wing area 44.08 m² (474.5 sq ft)
Weights: Empty 11,340 kg (25,000 lb); MTOW 18,144 kg (40,000 lb)
Performance: Maximum speed 2,230 km/h (1,203 knots) Mach 2.1 at 10,975 m (36,000 ft); operational ceiling 17,375 m (57,000 ft); radius 972 km (604 miles)
Load: Two Red Top missiles, plus two 30 mm Aden cannon

An English Electric Lightning F.Mk 53

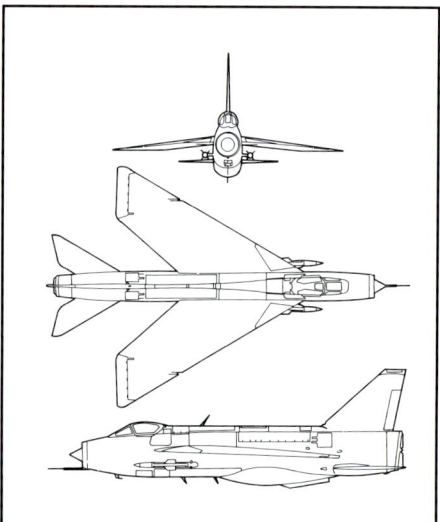

Lightning F.Mk 6

JET FIGHTERS

MCDONNELL DOUGLAS F-4 PHANTOM II (U.S.A.)

IAI F-4 Phantom 2000

In October 1979, the 5,057th Phantom II was completed, ending the West's largest warplane production programme since World War II. The programme was devoted to an exceptional type that must be numbered in the five most important warplanes of all time. It was planned initially as an all-weather attack aircraft, but then adapted during design into an all-weather fleet-defence and tactical fighter. The first of two XF4H-1 prototypes flew in May 1958 with early examples of the equally classic J79 afterburning turbojet. The 45 F4H-1Fs (later F-4As) were really pre-production types with 7326-kg (16,150-lb) thrust J79-GE-2/2A engines.

True operational capability came with 649 F4H-1 (later F-4B) with 7711-kg (17,000-lb) thrust J79-GE-8 engines, 46 RF-4B reconnaissance aircraft for the U.S. Marine Corps, 635 F-4C (originally F-110A) attack fighters for the U.S. Air Force with 7711-kg (17,000-lb) thrust J79-GE-15 engines, 499 RF-4C USAF tactical reconnaissance aircraft, 773 F-4Ds based on the F-4C but with electronics tailored to USAF rather than U.S. Navy requirements, 1,405 F-4Es for the USAF with 8119-kg (17,900-lb) thrust J79-GE-17 engines, improved radar, leading-edge slats and an internal 20-mm rotary-barrel cannon, 175 F-4F air-superiority fighters for West Germany, 512 F-4Js for the U.S. Navy with 8119-kg (17,900-lb) thrust J79-GE-10 engines, a revised wing and modified tail, 52 F-4Ks based on the F-4J for the Royal Navy with Rolls-Royce Spey turbofans, and 118 F-4Ms based on the F-4K for the Royal Air Force.

There have been several other versions produced by converting older airframes with more advanced electronics as well as other features, such as the similar F-4N and F-4S developments of the F-4B and F-4J for the U.S. Navy, the F-4G for the USAF's 'Wild Weasel' radar-suppression role, and the Super Phantom (or Phantom 2000) rebuild of the F-4E by Israel Aircraft Industries.

McDONNELL DOUGLAS F-4E PHANTOM II
Role: All-weather strike fighter
Crew/Accommodation: Two
Power Plant: Two 8,119 kgp (17,900 lb s.t.) General Electric J79-GE-17 turbojets with reheat
Dimensions: Span 11.71 m (38.42 ft); length 19.2 m (63 ft); wing area 49.2 m² (530 sq ft)
Weights: Empty 13,397 kg (29,535 lb); MTOW 27,965 kg (61,651 lb)
Performance: Maximum speed 2,390 km/h (1,290 knots) Mach 2.2 at 12,190 m (40,000 ft); operational ceiling 18,975 m (62,250 ft); radius 960 km (518 naut. miles) typical combat mission
Load: One 20 mm multi-barrel cannon and four medium-range air-to-air missiles, plus up to 7,257 kg (16,000 lb) of externally carried weapons or fuel

The RF-4C is a version of the McDonnell Douglas Phantom II land-based fighter series

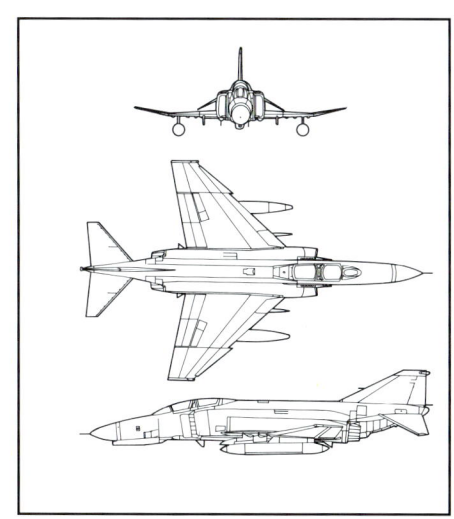

F-4E Phantom II

NORTHROP F-5 Family (U.S.A.)

F-5E Tiger II

The F-5 Freedom Fighter was developed, using U.S. Government funding, from Northrop's private-venture N-156 design as a modestly supersonic fighter and attack aircraft with the light weight, compact dimensions and simple avionics that would make it suitable for export under the U.S.'s 'Military Assistance Programs', or for sale to other forces requiring an uncomplicated jet. The concept's first concrete expression was the N-156T supersonic trainer that first flew in April 1959 as the YT-38 with two 953-kg (2,600-lb) thrust General Electric J85-GE-1 non-afterburning turbojets, though the third to sixth prototypes had the 1,633-kg (3,600-lb) afterburning thrust J85-GE-5 engines that paved the way for the 1,746-kg (3,850-lb) thrust J85-GE-5As used in the T-38A Talon version, of which 1,189 were built (including the two prototypes), most going to USAF training establishments; in 1999 many hundreds remain flying and are undergoing upgrade.

The N-156F fighter was developed in F-5A single-seat and F-5B two-seat variants, and first flew in July 1959 with 1,850-kg (4,850-lb) thrust J85-GE-13 turbojets. Production of the F-5A and F-5B totalled 818 and 290 respectively for various countries in differently designated versions that included the Canadair-built CF-5 for Canada, NF-5 for the Netherlands, F-5G for Norway and the CASA-built SF-5 for Spain. There was also an RF-5A reconnaissance model. The mantle of the Freedom Fighter was then assumed by the more capable Tiger II variant produced in F-5E single-seat and F-5F two-seat forms with an integrated fire-control system as well as 2,268-kg (5,000-lb) thrust J85-GE-21 engines and aerodynamic refinements for much improved payload and performance.

The F-5E first flew in August 1972 and deliveries of Tiger IIs began in 1973. Large-scale production followed in the U.S.A. and abroad (including Switzerland and Taiwan), and by the close of production Tiger IIs had raised the overall F-5 production total to well over 2,600 aircraft, including a small number of RF-5E TigerEye reconnaissance aircraft.

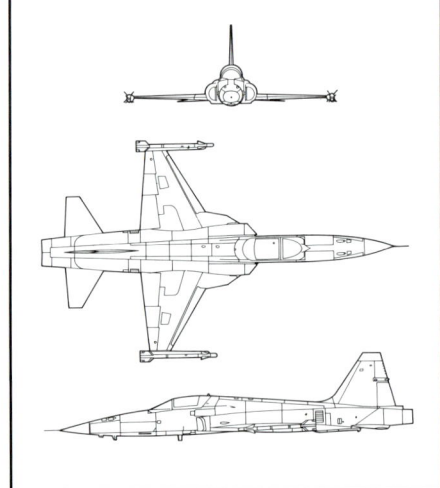

Northrop F-5E Tiger II

NORTHROP F-5E TIGER II
Role: Strike fighter
Crew/Accommodation: One
Power Plant: Two 2,268 kgp (5,000 lb s.t.) General Electric J85-GE-21 turbojets with reheat
Dimensions: Span 8.13 m (26.66 ft); length 14.68 m (48.16 ft); wing area 17.3 m² (186.2 sq ft)
Weights: Empty 4,392 kg (9,683 lb); MTOW 11,195 kg (24,680 lb)
Performance: Maximum speed 1,730 km/h (934 knots) Mach 1.63 at 11,000 m (36,090 ft); operational ceiling 15,790 m (51,800 ft); radius 222 km (138 miles) with full warload
Load: Two 20 mm cannon, plus up to 3,175 kg (7,000 lb) of ordnance, including two short-range air-to-air missiles

The Northrop F-5F Tiger II became the two-seat version of the F-5E single-seater

MIKOYAN MiG-25 'FOXBAT' Series (U.S.S.R.)

MiG-25 'Foxbat'

The MiG-25 was designed to provide the Soviets with an interceptor capable of dealing with the United States' North American B-70 Valkyrie Mach 3 high-altitude strategic bomber. When the B-70 was cancelled, the Soviets continued to develop this very high-performance interceptor which first flew as the Ye-266 in 1964. The type is built largely of stainless steel with titanium leading edges to deal with friction-generated heat at Mach 3, but at such a speed is virtually incapable of manoeuvre.

The type entered service in 1972 with valve-technology radar that lacked the sophistication of then current Western equipments but offered very high power, and thus the ability to 'burn through' the defences provided by the enemy's electronic counter-measures. Variants became the 'Foxbat-A' interceptor with four air-to-air missiles, the 'Foxbat-B' operational-level reconnaissance bomber, the 'Foxbat-C' two-seat conversion trainer, and the 'Foxbat-D' improved reconnaissance aircraft.

As 'Foxbat-A' became obsolete, two further combat versions were developed, as 'Foxbat-E', with much-improved radar (both newly built and by conversion of 'Foxbat-A's) and 'Foxbat-F' for an air-defence suppression role with a specialized radar-warning suite and AS-11 'Kilter' anti-radar missiles. Russian interceptors were withdrawn by 1994, although others were used abroad, but reconnaissance versions remain operational. The MiG-31 'Foxhound' entered service in 1983 as a development of the MiG-25 with greater power and the combination of electronically-scanned phased array radar with multi-target capability, improved missiles (mainly to protect against cruise missile attack) and longer range/duration. Maximum speed is Mach 2.83.

MIKOYAN MIG-25 'FOXBAT-B'
Role: High speed reconnaissance-bomber
Crew/Accommodation: One
Power Plant: Two 11,200-kgp (24,700-lb s.t.) Soyuz/Tumansky R-15B turbojets with reheat
Dimensions: Span 13.38 m (43.9 ft); length 21.55 m (70.7 ft); wing area 61.4 m² (660.9 sq ft)
Weights: MTOW 41,200 kg (90,830 lb)
Performance: Maximum speed 3,006 km/h (1,868 mph) at 13,000m (42,630 ft); operational ceiling 23,000 m (75,460 ft); range 2,400 km (1,491 miles) with 4 bombs and a drop-tank
Load: 5,000 kg (11,023 lb) of bombs

Mikoyan MiG-25 'Foxbat-A'

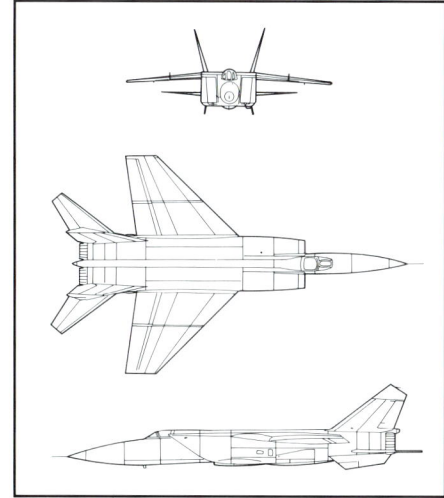

MiG-25 'Foxbat-A'

MIKOYAN MiG-23 and MiG-27 'FLOGGER' Series (U.S.S.R.)

MiG-27 'Flogger'

In 1967, the MiG bureau flew its 23-11 swing-wing fighter prototype for evaluation against the 23-01 tailed-delta prototype powered by a single Tumansky R-27-300 turbojet propulsion engine and given V/STOL capability by the incorporation of two Kolesov RD36-35 lift jets in the centre of the fuselage. The 23-11 proved superior, and as the MiG-23 was produced between 1969 and 1985 for Soviet use and export, with 5,047 completed. 'Flogger-A' was given one Tumansky R-27 engine and Sapfir-21 radar, but 'Flogger-B' introduced the R-29 engine and Sapfir-23 'High Lark' radar, plus other improvements and become the standard basic production version. Other versions followed, including 'Flogger-Fard H' as ground-attack variants with Lyulka or Tumansky engines, mainly for export. The final variant was known in the West as 'Flogger-K', an upgrade with vortex generators at the wingroots and nose probe, a radar suited to close-air combat, AA-11 'Archer' missiles and more. The MiG-27 first flew in 1970 as a supersonic dedicated attack derivative of the MiG-23 with a revised forward fuselage offering heavy armour protection and fitted with terrain-avoidance rather than search radar. The MiG-27 also has a less advanced powerplant with fixed inlets and a simple nozzle for its reduced-performance role at low altitude; special target-acquisition and weapon guidance equipment are installed, as are a multi-barrel cannon and additional hardpoints for the larger offensive load. Two variants became the 'Flogger-D' and 'Flogger-J'.

MiG-23 'Flogger-B'

MIKOYAN MIG-27 'FLOGGER-J'
Role: Ground attack with variable geometry wing
Crew/Accommodation: One
Power Plant: One 11,500-kgp (25,350-lb s.t.) Soyuz R-29B-300 turbofan with reheat
Dimensions: Span 13.97 m (45.8 ft), swept 7.78 m (25.5 ft); length 17.08 m (56 ft); wing area 27.26 m² (293.42 sq ft)
Weights: Empty 12,100 kg (26,676 lb); MTOW 18,100 kg (39,900 lb)
Performance: Maximum speed 1,350 km/h (839 mph) Mach 1.1 at sea level; operational ceiling 13,000+ m (46,650+ ft); radius 540 km (336 miles) with two missiles and three drop-tanks
Load: One 30-mm cannon, plus up to 3,000 kg (6,614 lb) of weapons.

This 'Flogger-D' was given terrain-avoidance radar

SAAB 37 VIGGEN (Sweden)

JA 37 Viggen

With the Saab 37 Viggen (Thunderbolt), first flown in February 1967, Sweden produced a true multi-role fighter with a thrust-reversible afterburning turbofan and a canard layout for true STOL capability using short lengths of road as emergency airstrips. The type was designed around the integrated weapon system concept pioneered in the United States, with power based on a Swedish licence-built version of the Pratt & Whitney JT8D turbofan but fitted in this application with Swedish-designed afterburning and thrust-reversing units. The advanced electronics include pulse-Doppler radar, a head-up display and other items linked by a digital fire-control system to maximize the type's offensive and defensive capabilities with effective weapons and electronic countermeasures.

Production totalled 329, and the variants have been the AJ 37 attack aircraft with the 11,790-kg (25,992-lb) thrust RM8A, the SF 37 overland reconnaissance aircraft with a modified nose accommodating seven cameras and an infa-red sensor, the SH 37 overwater reconnaissance aircraft with search radar, and the SK 35 tandem two-seat operational trainer with a taller vertical tail. A 'Viggen Mk 2' development became the JA 37 interceptor with the 12,750-kg (28,109-lb) thrust RM8B turbofan, a number of airframe modifications, an underfuselage pack housing the extremely potent Oerlikon-Bührle KCA 30-mm cannon, together with a revised electronic suite with much improved radar. Finally, 75 AJ/SH/SFs were converted between 1993 and 1995 to AJS 37s, given more modern computers and other avionics, plus new reconnaissance equipment and new weapon choices, allowing any aircraft to perform air defence, attack or reconnaissance roles.

SAAB JA 37 VIGGEN
Role: Interceptor
Crew/Accommodation: One
Power Plant: One 12,750 khp (28,109 lb s.t.) Volvo Flyg motor RM8B turbofan with reheat
Dimensions: Span 10.6 m (34.78 ft); length 16.4 m (53.8 ft); wing area 46 m² (495.1 sq ft)
Weights: Empty 12,200 kg (26,455 lb); MTOW 20,000 kg (44,090 lb)
Performance: Maximum speed 2,231 km/h (1,386 mph) Mach 2.10 at 11,000 m (36.090 ft); operational ceiling 18,000 m (59,050ft); radius 500 km (311 miles)
Load: One 30-mm cannon, plus up to 6,000 kg (13,277 lb) of externally-carried weapons/fuel, including two medium-range and four short-range air-to-air missiles

The SH 37 is the overwater reconnaissance variant of the Saab Viggen family

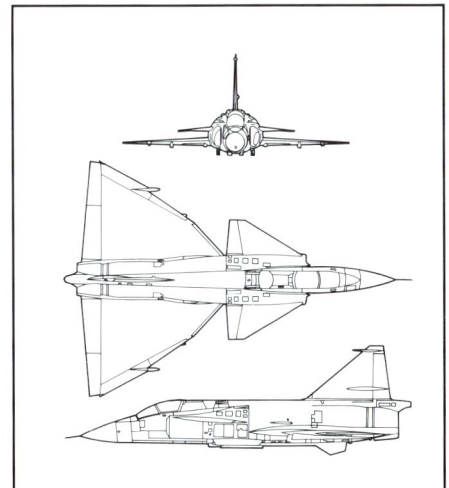

Saab AJ 37 Viggen

GRUMMAN F-14 TOMCAT (U.S.A.)

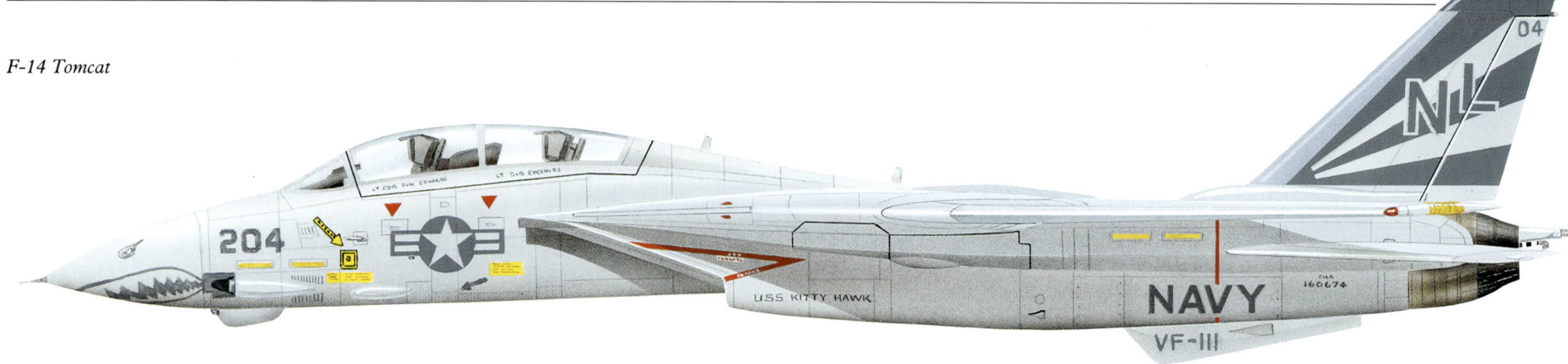

F-14 Tomcat

After the cancellation of the F-111B, developed primarily by Grumman as the fleet defence fighter equivalent of the General Dynamics F-111A land-based interdictor, the U.S. Navy issued a requirement for a new fighter. Submissions were received from five companies, but Grumman had a headstart with its G-303 design that made valuable use of the company's experience of variable-geometry wings, and also incorporated the F-111B's TF30 engines, AIM-54 Phoenix long-range air-to-air missiles, and AWG-9 radar fire-control system. In January 1969, the G-303 was selected for development as the F-14, and the first of 12 YF-14A pre-production aircraft flew in December 1970. The Tomcat was aerodynamically more tractable because of its 'glove vanes', small surfaces extending from the leading-edge roots of the main wings' fixed structure as the outer surfaces swept aft, which regulated movement in the centre of pressure to reduce pitch alterations.

The F-14A initial model entered service in October 1972 and immediately proved itself a classic fighter of its type in terms of performance, manoeuvrability, and weapon system capability. Some aircraft have been adapted for the reconnaissance role as the F-14A/TARPS with a ventral equipment pod. The only limitation to the F-14's total success was the powerplant of two 9480-kg (20,900-lb) thrust Pratt & Whitney TF30-P-412-A turbofans, which were not designed for fighter use and therefore lack the flexibility required for this role. For F-14As built after 1984, the TF30-P-414A was introduced, while F-14Bs and Ds produced by manufacture and conversion have 12,247-kg (27,000-lb) thrust General Electric F110-GE-400 turbofans. In addition, many F-14s have been given LANTIRN infra-red pods to permit FAC and strike missions, nicknamed 'Bombats'. Iran also received F-14s

GRUMMAN F-14A TOMCAT
Role: Carrier fighter, attack and reconnaissance
Crew/Accommodation: Two
Power Plant: Two 9480-kg (20,900 lb) thrust Pratt & Whitney TF30-P-412A turbofans
Dimensions: Span unswept 19.6 m (64.1 ft), swept 11.7 m (38.2 ft); length 19.1 m (62.7 ft); wing area 52.5 m² (565 sq ft)
Weights: Empty 17,650 kg (38,910 lb); MTOW 33,725 kg (74,350 lb)
Performance: Maximum speed 2,498 km/h (1,552 mph), Mach 2.34 at 11.276 m (37,000 ft); operational ceiling 19,500 m (64,000 ft); typical range for air-to-air mission 852 km (530 miles)
Load: Up to 6,577 kg (14,500 lb) with typically 4 AIM-54C Phoenix and 2 AIM-9 Sidewinders, plus an internal 6-barrel 20-mm General Electric M61 Vulcan cannon. F-14D can carry AMRAAM AAMs

Grumman F-14A Tomcat

A Grumman F-14A Tomcat in the markings of US Naval Aviation

DASSAULT MIRAGE F1 (France)

Mirage F1C

The Mirage F1 was developed as a successor to the Mirage III/5 family, but is a markedly different aircraft with 'conventional' flying surfaces. The French government originally wanted a two-seat warplane, and such a type was evolved by the company as the Mirage F2, powered by a SNECMA/Pratt & Whitney TF306 turbofan. At the same time the company worked as a private venture on the Mirage F1, a smaller and lighter single-seater sized to the SNECMA Atar turbojet.

The Mirage F2 flew in June 1966, but cost too much for a profitable production contract. The Mirage F1 first flew in December 1966 with the Atar 09K-31 turbojet. After the Mirage F2 programme was cancelled the French government ordered three pre-production examples of the Mirage F1. These displayed excellent performance and overall capabilities as multi-role warplanes, their primary advantages over the Mirage III/5 family being larger warload, easy handling at low altitude, good rate of climb, and 40 per cent greater fuel capacity (through the use of integral rather than bladder tanks) all combined with semi-STOL field performance thanks to the use of droopable leading edges and large trailing-edge flaps on the sharply swept wing, which is mounted in the shoulder position.

The Mirage F1 was ordered into production with the Atar 09K-50 afterburning turbojet. Like the preceding Mirage III/5 series, the Mirage F1 has been a considerable (if not outstanding) commercial success. The main variants have been the Mirage F1A clear-weather ground-attack fighter, the Mirage F1B and D two-seat trainers, the Mirage F1C (and Mirage F1C-200 long-range) multi-role all-weather interceptor with attack capability, the Mirage F1E multi-role export fighter, and the Mirage F1CR-200 long-range reconnaissance aircraft. Some French F1C-200s have been adapted as Mirage F1CTs, basically to F1E standard.

Dassault Mirage F1 CTs (SIRPA Air)

DASSAULT MIRAGE F1CT
Role: Strike fighter
Crew/Accommodation: One
Power Plant: One 7,900 kgp (15,873 lb) SNECMA Atar 09K-50 turbojets with reheat
Dimensions: Span 8.4 m (27.55 ft); length 15.3 m (50.2 ft); wing area 25 m² (270 sq ft)
Weights: Empty 7,400 kg (16,315 lb); MTOW 16,200 kg (35,700 lb)
Performance: Maximum speed 2,335 km/h (1,450 mph) Mach 2.2 at 12.000 m (39,370 ft); operational ceiling 20,000 m (65,600 ft) radius of action 425 km (264 miles) with 3,500 kg attack load
Load: Two 30-mm DEFA cannon, plus up to 6,300 kg (13,890 lb) of externally carried weapons

Dassault Mirage F1C

BOEING (McDONNELL DOUGLAS) F-15 EAGLE (U.S.A.)

F-15C Eagle

The F-15 was planned as the U.S. Air Force's successor to the F-4 in the air superiority role. After three years of design studies the type was selected for hardware development in December 1969. The first of two YF-15A prototypes emerged for its first flight in July 1972 as a massive aircraft with two 10,809-kg (23,830-lb) thrust Pratt & Whitney F100-P-100 turbofans, sophisticated aerodynamics, advanced electronics including the APG-63 multi-role radar and a pilot's head-up display, and the world's first production cockpit of the HOTAS (Hands-On-Throttle-And-Stick) type.

The Eagle entered service in November 1974, and has since proved itself a first-class and versatile warplane. Its powerful engines allow the type to carry a large weight of widely assorted weapons in the primary air-to-air and secondary air-to-ground roles, and also generate a thrust-weight ratio in the order of unity for an exceptionally high rate of climb and very good manoeuvrability. The initial F-15A single-seat model was complemented by the F-15B (originally TF-15A) two-seat combat-capable version.

In 1979 production switched to the F-15C and F-15D respectively. These are powered by 10,637-kg (23,450-lb) thrust F100-P-220 engines, and have more advanced systems, including the improved APG-70 radar from 1985 production onward, as well as provision for external carriage of the so-called FAST (Fuel and Sensor Tactical) packs that provide considerably more fuel and weapons at a negligible increase in drag and weight. The F-15C and D are built under licence in Japan as the F-15J and F-15DJ. In 1988 the USAF received its first example of the F-15E, airframe (though strengthened) and offering advanced air-to-air capability combined with ground attack. In 1989 the first flight took place of the F-15 SMTD, an experimental vectored-thrust conversion of an F-15B, with two dimensional nozzles and foreplanes.

F-15E Eagle

McDONNELL DOUGLAS F-15E EAGLE
Role: All-weather strike fighter
Crew/Accommodation: Two
Power Plant: Two 10,782 kgp (23,770 lb s.t.) Pratt & Whitney F100-PW-220 turbofans with reheat
Dimensions: Span 13.05 m (42 ft); length 19.45 m (63.79 ft); wing area 56.5 m² (608 sq ft)
Weights: Empty 14,515 kg (32,000 lb); MTOW 36,741 kg (81,000 lb)
Performance: Maximum speed 2,698 km/h (1,675 mph); operational ceiling 18,300 m (60,000 ft); radius of action 1,271 km (790 miles)
Load: Up to 11,113 kg (24,500 lb) of weaponry, and one 20-mm multi-barrel cannon mounted internally

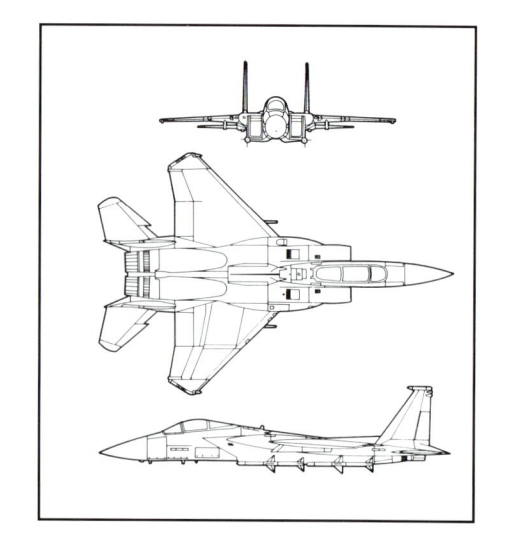

McDonnell Douglas F-15C Eagle

LOCKHEED MARTIN F-16 FIGHTING FALCON (U.S.A.)

JET FIGHTERS

F-16A Fighting Falcon

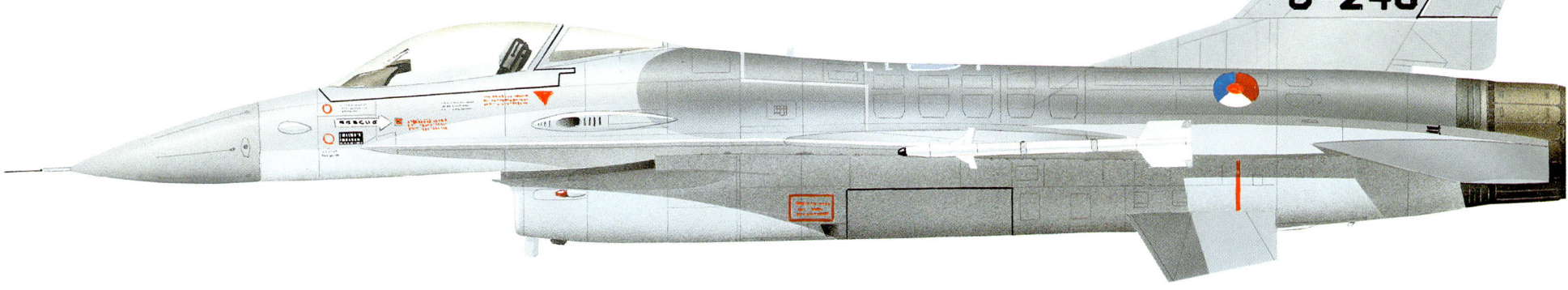

During the Vietnam War the United States Air Force discovered that its fighters were in general handicapped by their very large size, weight and Mach 2 performance, all of which were liabilities that seriously eroded reliability and combat agility in the type of turning dogfight that became increasingly common at low and medium altitudes. To help to find a solution to this problem, in 1971 the U.S. Air Force instituted a Light-Weight Fighter competition for a low cost day fighter, and General Dynamics produced its Model 401 design.

The first of two YF-16 prototypes flew in January 1974, and 12 months later the type was declared winner of the LWF competition. The basic type was adopted as the U.S. Air Force's Air-Combat Fighter, but its role was greatly expanded to include ground attack and, because of provision for radar and upgraded navigation equipment, all-weather operations. In June 1975 it was announced that the same type had been adopted by a four-nation European consortium. The first production models were the single-seat F-16A and two-seat F-16B, which entered service in January 1979 and received the name Fighting Falcon in 1980. Since then, the type has gone on to become numerically the most important fighter in the Western world, with nearly 4,000 delivered to many countries. The type is based on blended contours and relaxed stability, the latter controlled by a fly-by-wire system. The pilot controls the fighter using a sidestick joystick 'controller', and occupies a 30° reclining ejection seat that assists in helping the pilot withstand high 'g' forces.

Many structural and electronic improvements, including a more capable radar, created the current F-16C single-seat and F-16D two-seat variants, which can again use either General Electric or Pratt & Whitney engines in their most recent and powerful forms. Other variants produced for specific missions or experimental use includes the USAF's F-16HTS (F-16Cs) for SEAD (suppression of enemy air defenses) and F-16CAS for close air support and battlefield interdiction.

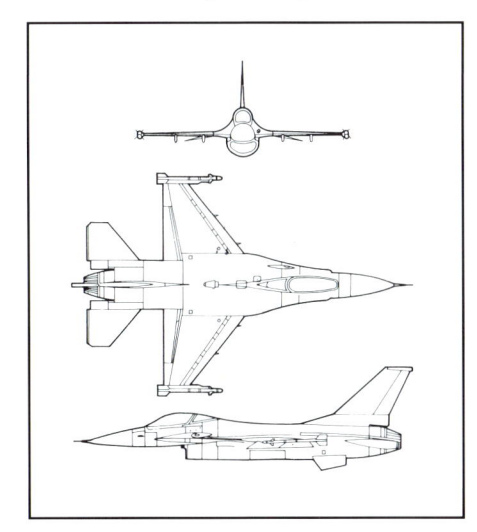

F-16C Fighting Falcon

LOCKHEED MARTIN F-16C FIGHTING FALCON
Role: Air dominance and ground attack fighter
Crew/Accommodation: One
Power Plant: One 13,154 kgp (29,000 lb s.t.) General Electric F110-GE-129 or 13,200 kgp (29,100 lb s.t.) Pratt & Whitney F100-PW-229 in current Block 50/52 F-16Cs
Dimensions: Span 10 m (32.79 ft); length 15.02 m (49.3 ft); wing area 17.87 m² (300 sq ft)
Weights: Empty 8,753 kg (18,900 lb); MTOW 19,187 kg (42,300 lb)
Performance: Maximum speed 2,146 km/h (1,335 mph) Mach 2.02 at 12,190 m (40,000 ft); operational ceiling over 15,240 m (50,000 ft); radius of action 1,605 km (997 miles) with four air-to-air missiles and maximum internal fuel and 3,936 litres in drop-tanks
Load: One 20-mm cannon, plus up to 7,071–7,225 kg (15,590–15,930 lb) of other weapons

F-16C Fighting Falcon, formerly a General Dynamics product

BOEING F/A-18 HORNET Family (U.S.A.)

F/A-18A Hornet

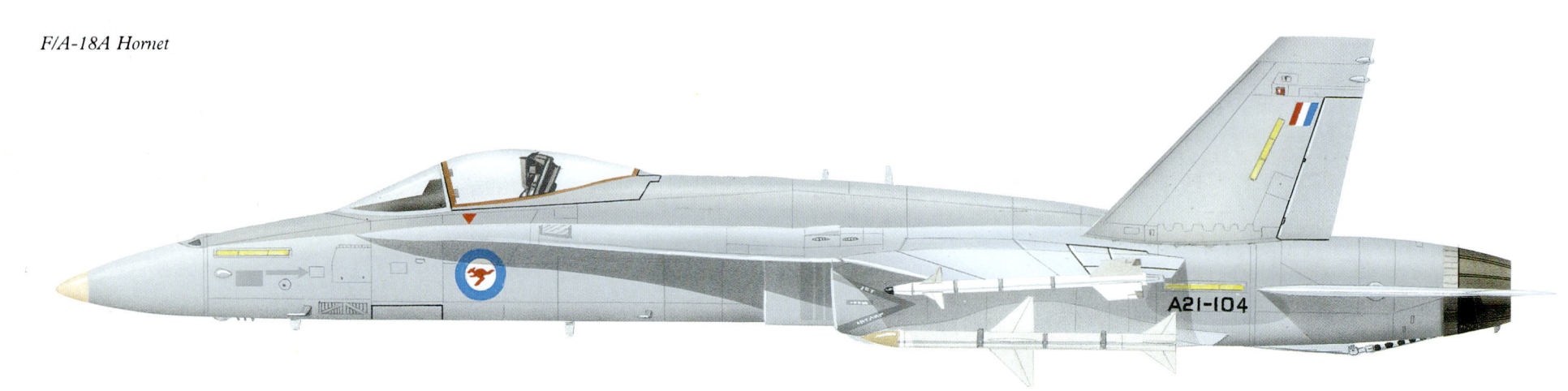

Serving with the U.S. Navy and Marine Corps as replacement for the F-4 and A-7 in the fighter and attack roles respectively, the dual-capability F/A-18 is one of the West's most important carrierborne warplanes, and has also secured useful export orders for land-based use. Originally a McDonnell Douglas product (before the company's merger with Boeing in 1997), the type was derived from the Northrop YF-17 (losing contender to the YF-16 in the USAF's Light-Weight Fighter competition) in order to meet the requirements of the Navy Air Combat Fighter requirement.

In the development programme undertaken by Northrop and McDonnell Douglas, the YF-17 was enlarged, aerodynamically refined, re-engined and fitted with advanced mission electronics. The Hornet prototype first flew in November 1978. Initial plans to procure separate F-18 and A-18 fighter and attack variants had been abandoned when it was realized that different software in the mission computers would allow a single type to be optimized in each role. McDonnell Douglas assumed production leadership, and the F/A-18s entered service late in 1983 as the F/A-18A single-seater and its combat-capable two-seat partner, the F/A-18B, originally designated the TF/A-18A.

The F/A-18A was replaced in production by the F/A-18C in 1987 with a number of electronic and system improvements and the ability to carry more advanced weapons. The two-seat equivalent became the F/A-18D. Night attack capability was added to C/Ds from the 139th aircraft delivered since 1989. Also, 31 USMC F/A-18Ds began entering service as F/A-18D (RC)s in 1999 for reconnaissance. Meanwhile, in November 1995, the F/A-18E Super Hornet prototype first flew, and deliveries to the U.S. Navy have begun of 'E' single-seaters and 'F' two-seaters, offering more power, greater range and payload, improved avionics and more.

F/A-18A Hornet

McDonnell Douglas F/A-18C Hornet
Role: Naval and land-based strike fighter
Crew/Accommodation: One
Power Plant: Two 7,257 kgp (16,000 lb s.t.) General Electric F404-GE-400 turbofans with reheat, or more powerful GE-402s from 1992
Dimensions: Span 11.4 m (36.5 ft); length 17.1 m (56 ft); wing area 37.16 m² (400 sq ft)
Weights: Empty 10,810 kg (23,832 lb); MTOW 25,401 kg (56,000 lb)
Performance: Maximum speed over Mach 1.8; operational ceiling 15,240 m (50,000 ft); radius 740 km (461miles) with missiles and sinternal fuel only
Load: One 20-mm multi-barrel cannon plus up to 7,030 kg (15,500lb of weapons, including up to 10 AMRAAM and two Sidewinder missiles or a mix of AAMS and attack weapons

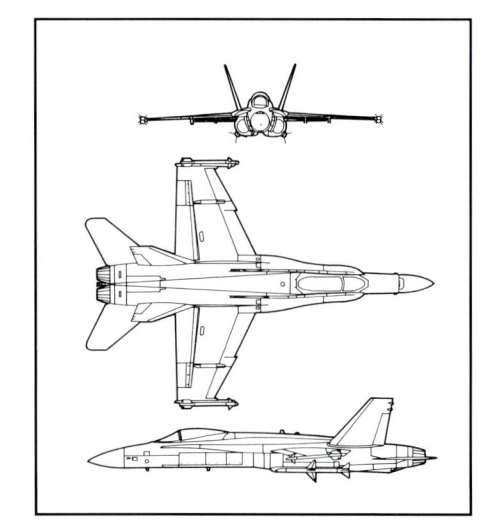

F/A-18A Hornet

JET FIGHTERS

MAPO 'MiG' MiG-29 'FULCRUM' Family (Russia)

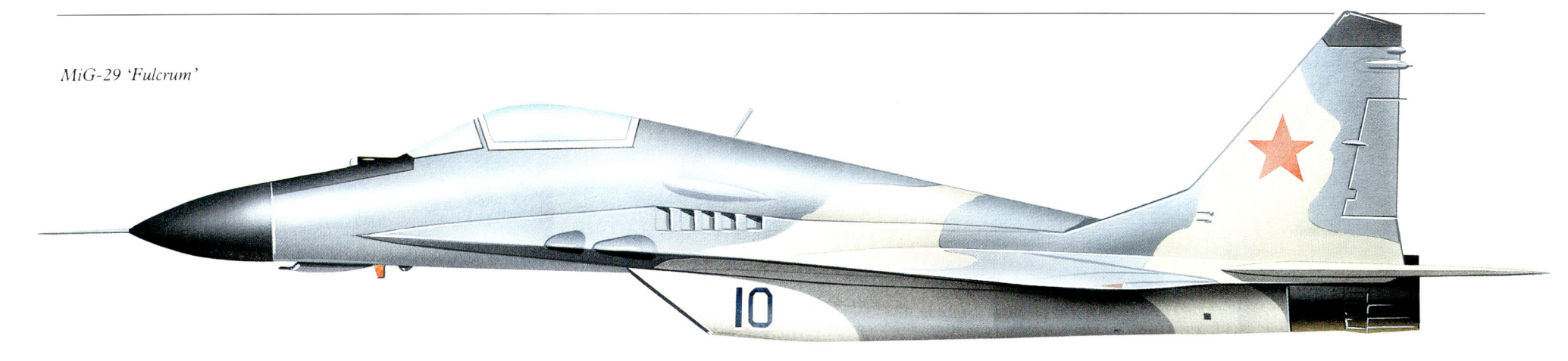

MiG-29 'Fulcrum'

First flown in October 1977 and delivered to the Soviet air force from 1983, the MiG-29 is also known by the NATO reporting name 'Fulcrum' and is a lightweight close-air fighter optimized for air combat but with a secondary attack capability. Despite its use of a conventional mechanical control system in an airframe of very advanced but basically conventional configuration, the type possesses great agility. Moreover, a genuine look-down/shoot-down capability is offered by the combination of a radar that can track up to ten targets simultaneously and engage one or two, and use of AA-10 'Alamo' snap-down air-to-air missiles. The 'Fulcrum-A' has undergone a number of changes since it was first seen, the consensus being that these indicate a number of fixes to bring the design up to the present standard.

The first variant was probably a pre-production model and carried small detachable ventral tail fins reminiscent of those carried by the Sukhoi Su-27 'Flanker'. Later 'Fulcrum-A's introduced extended-chord rudders. The MiG-29UB 'Fulcrum-B' became the two-seat combat-capable conversion and continuation trainer derivative of the 'Fulcrum-A' with the radar removed, though a planned upgrade may restore radar to allow full multi-role capability. The next single-seater became 'Fulcrum-C', distinguishable by its larger dorsal fairing for carriage of an active ECM system and more internal fuel. An improved version of 'C' introduced better Topaz radar and added new AA-12 'Adder' missiles to the weapon choices. MiG-29M 'Fulcrum-E' has been under trial as a new tactical fighter and ground attack model with greatly enhanced capabilities, with export versions including the MiG-33, while MiG-29K has undergone trials as a naval version suited to aircraft carrier operations.

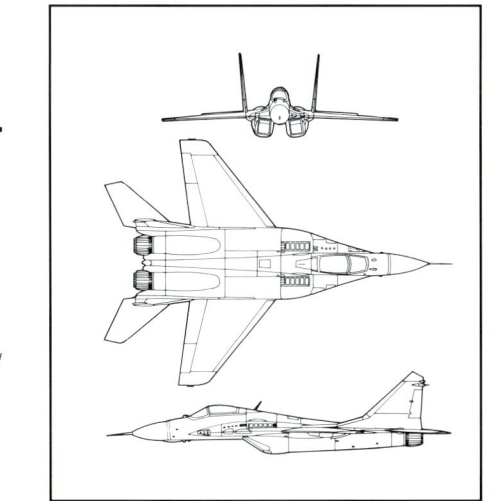

MiG-29 'Fulcrum-A'

MAPO 'MiG' MiG-29 'FULCRUM'
Role: Fighter
Crew/Accommodation: One
Power Plant: Two 8,300 kgp (18,300 lb s.t.) Klimov RD-33 turbofans with reheat
Dimensions: Span 11.36 m (37.27 ft); length 17.32 m (56.83 ft); wing area 38.1 m² (410 sq ft)
Weights: Empty 10,900 kg (24,030 lb); MTOW 18,480 kg (40,740 lb)
Performance: Maximum speed 2,440 km/h (1,516 mph Mach 2.3 at 11,000 m (36,090 ft); operational ceiling 17,500 m (57,400 ft); range 2,100 km (1,305 miles) maximum
Load: One 30-mm cannon plus about 4,000 kg (8,818 lb) of external weapons, typically 2 medium-range AA-10s and 4 AA-11 or AA-8 short-range missiles

MiG-29 'Fulcrum-A'

SUKHOI Su-27 'FLANKER' Family (Russia)

Su-27 'Flanker-A'

Developed during the 1970s as a long-range air-superiority fighter to match the U.S. Air Force's McDonnell Douglas F-15 Eagle, the Su-27 drew on similar aerodynamic research that assisted the MiG-29, but was designed to be inherently unstable because of the adoption of an analog fly-by-wire control system. First flown in May 1977, initial operational capability was achieved in December 1984. The first version became known to NATO as the 'Flanker-A', though referring to four prototypes and five pre-production aircraft with the vertical tail surfaces located centrally above the engine installations, rounded wingtips and mostly AL-21F3 engines.

The basic full-production version became the 'Flanker-B' with squared-off wingtips, plus a number of refinements such as leading edge slats and vertical tail surfaces located farther outboard. 'Flanker-B' has been built in Su-27S tactical and Su-27P air defence models.

Su-27UB 'Flanker-C' is a tandem two-seat combat trainer variant, first flown in production form in 1986. Although adding a second cockpit forced a reduction in fuel load, it retains full combat capability and has all the necessary radar and weapon systems.

From Su-27 has been developed a wide family of related warplanes. These include the Su-30 two-seat long-range multi-role interceptor that has extra avionics to lead a group of Su-27 fighters; Su-32FN with side-by-side seating for maritime strike and related Su-27IB/Su-34 for tactical interdiction; Su-33/Su-27K carrierborne fighter and anti-ship single-seater, known to NATO as 'Flanker-D' (also two-seat version); and Su-35 and Su-37 (or Su-27M) as fighter and ground attack aircraft, the Su-37 with thrust-vectoring nozzles.

Sukhoi Su-27 'Flanker-B'

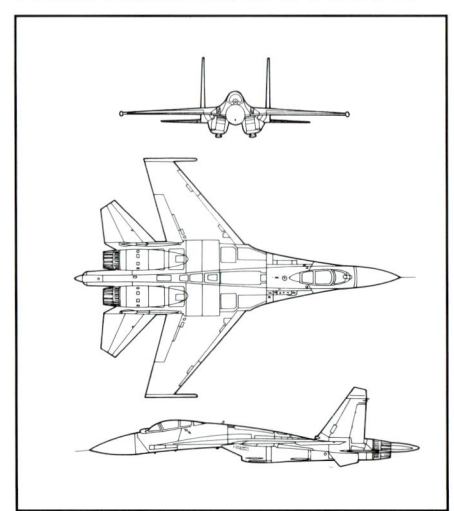

SUKHOI Su-27 'FLANKER B'
Role: Interceptor
Crew/Accommodation: One
Power Plant: Two 12,500 kgp (27,560 lb s.t.) Saturn AL-31F turbofans with reheat
Dimensions: Span 14.7 m (48.25 ft); length 21.94 m (72 ft); wing area 62.04 m² (667.8 sq ft)
Weights: Empty 16,380 kg (36,112 lb); MTOW 28,300 kg (62,390 lb)
Performance: Maximum speed 2,300 km/h (1,429 mph) Mach 2.17; operational ceiling 18,500 m (60,700 ft); range 2,800 km (1,740 miles)
Load: One 30-mm multi-barrel cannon plus up to 8,000 kg (17,636 lb) of weapons, including 10 air-to-air missiles (up to six AA-10 'Alamos'

A Sukhoi Su-27 'Flanker-B'

DASSAULT MIRAGE 2000 (France)

Mirage 2000C

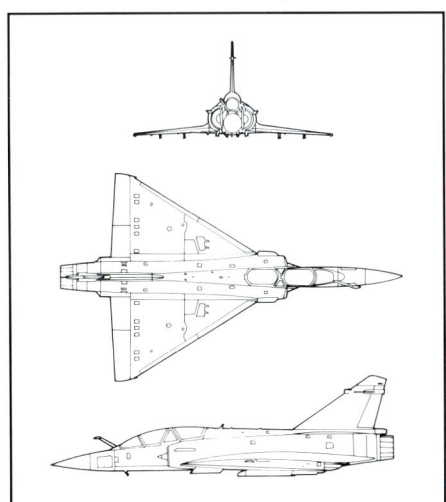

Mirage 2000-5

With the Mirage 2000 the manufacturer reverted to the delta-wing planform but, in this instance, of the relaxed-stability type with an electronic 'fly-by-wire' control system to avoid many of the low-level handling and tactical limitations suffered by the aerodynamically similar Mirage III/5 family. In the early and mid-1970s, Dassault was working on a prototype to meet the French air force's ACF (Avion de Combat Futur) requirement, but this was cancelled in 1975 when the service decided that a warplane powered by two SNECMA M53-3 turbofans was too large. In December 1975, therefore, the French government authorized the design and development of a smaller single-engined machine. This emerged as the Mirage 2000 with the 9,000-kg (19,840-lb) thrust SNECMA M53-5 turbofan in the smallest and lightest possible airframe for a high power/weight ratio.

The first of five prototypes flew during March 1978 and the prototypes soon demonstrated the Mirage 2000's complete superiority to the Mirage III in all flight regimes. The type remains in production, and the primary variants have been the Mirage 2000B two-seat operational trainer with a lengthened fuselage, the Mirage 2000C single-seat interceptor and multi-role fighter (now with the 9,700-kg (21,384-lb) thrust M53-P2 turbofan and RDI pulse Doppler radar in place of the original RDM multi-mode radar), the Mirage 2000N two-seat nuclear-capable strike fighter based on the airframe of the Mirage 2000B and optimized for low-level penetration, the Mirage 2000D based on 'N' and for all-weather attack, the Mirage 2000R single-seat reconnaissance fighter, the Mirage 2000E single-seat multi-role export derivative of the Mirage 2000C with RDM radar, the Mirage 2000ED training version of 'E' and the Mirage 2000-5 latest advanced multi-role combat aircraft for export and as some modified Mirage 2000Cs for French operation, with RDY radar capable of tracking up to 24 targets.

DASSAULT MIRAGE 2000C
Role: air superiority fighter
Crew/Accommodation: One
Power Plant: One 9,700 kgp (21,385 lb s.ts) SNECMA M53-P2 turbofan with reheat
Dimensions: Span 9.13 m (29.95 ft); length 14.36 m (47.1 ft); wing area 41 m² (441.3 sq ft)
Weights: Empty 7,500 kg (16,534 lb); MTOW 17,000 kg (37,480 lb)
Performance: Maximum speed 2,335 kn/h (1,450 mph) Mach 2.2 at 11,000m (36,000 ft); operational ceiling 18,000 m (60,000 ft); range 3,335 km (2,072 miles) with external fuel and four 250 kg bombs
Load: Two 30-mm DEFA cannon plus up to 6,300 kg (13,890 lb) of weapons including two Matra Magic 2 and two Matra Super 530D missiles

Mirage 2000C

SAAB AB GRIPEN JAS 39 (SWEDEN)

The Gripen is Sweden's very latest multi-role warplane, and is generally acknowledged to be the world's first production combat aircraft of the new fourth generation. It was developed and is being built by a Swedish industrial group in which SAAB is the largest partner in terms of programme value. Such is the potential of the aircraft that British Aerospace became a partner for joint marketing, adapting and supporting the Gripen on the export market.

Although a fairly small nation, Sweden has never compromised on its military aircraft, deciding its needs and building accordingly, even without the backing of export orders, though Gripen may well prove internationally successful. Another Swedish tradition has been to produce a single aircraft capable of fulfilling many roles through the adoption of specifically-equipped variants, while Swedish aircraft also have the ability to disperse to and operate from short sections of the nation's main road network in an emergency. With Gripen, the concept has been taken a stage further by having advanced computer systems so that each single Gripen can fully perform in any of the required fighter, attack and reconnaissance roles with the same pilot at any time, merely by selecting the system function and thereby the characteristics required to undertake that mission.

As a lightweight combat aircraft intended to eventually replace Viggens and Drakens in Swedish service, development of Gripen began in 1980 with a project definition phase. Full development started in June 1982, with the signing of a contract for five test aircraft and the first thirty production aircraft (Batch 1). The first flight of a test aircraft was achieved on 9 December 1988 and the Gripen joined the Air Force in 1996, first going to F7 Wing. The final Gripen of Batch 1 (30 aircraft) was delivered in December 1996, when deliveries of Batch 2 aircraft (including JAS 39B two-seat operational trainers) began to the Swedish Defence Material Administration. Batch 2 covered 96 single-seaters and 14 two-seaters, equipped with upgraded avionics software and new flight control system hardware, while in 1997 a third batch was ordered (64 aircraft). Eventually, twelve of the Air Force's thirteen squadrons will operate Gripens.

Gripen has rear-mounted delta wings and close-coupled all-moving canards, and uses a flight-by-wire flight control system. Strong but light carbonfibre has been used in the construction of about a third of the airframe. Remarkably, Gripen can be refuelled, rearmed, and essential servicing and inspections made in a turnaround time of under ten minutes by a technician and five conscripts under combat conditions

Gripen in F7 Wing markings, carrying wingtip Sidewinders, two underwing AGM-65 Maverick missiles and a drop tank

---

JAS 39A GRIPEN
Role: Multi-role fighter, attack, maritime attack and reconnaissance
Crew/Accommodation: One
Power Plant: One 8,212 kgp (18.105 lb s.t.) Volvo RM12 with reheat
Dimensions: Span 8.4 m (27.56 ft); length 14.1 m (46.26 ft);
Weights: Empty 6,620 kg (14,600 lb); MTOW 14,000 kg (30,865 lb)
Performance: Supersonic at all heights; radius of action 800 km (497 miles)
Load: One 27-mm Mauser cannon. Pylons on each wingtip (two), under the wings (four), under the air intakes (two) and under the fuselage (one) for a selection of weapons and stores that can include Sidewinder, AMRAAM or operational Mica air-to-air missiles, anti-ship, air-to-surface or other missiles, cluster weapons, rockets or other types.

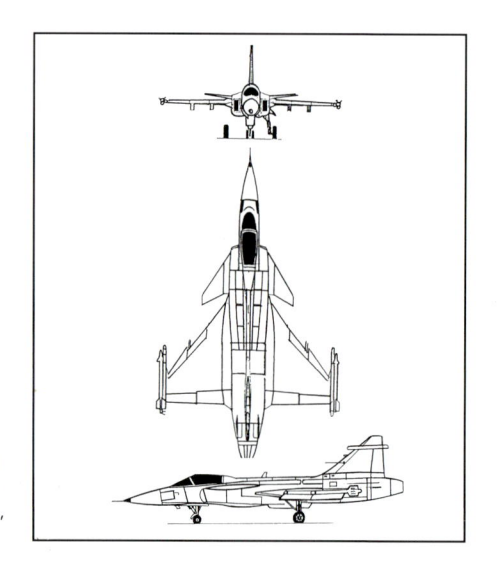

JAS 39 Gripen

JET FIGHTERS

LOCKHEED MARTIN F-22 RAPTOR (U.S.A.)

YF-22A Raptor

First F-22 Raptor EMD test aircraft

In late April 1991 the U.S. Air Force Secretary announced the selection of the Lockheed/Boeing/General Dynamics team to develop the Advanced Tactical Fighter (ATF) as the replacement for the F-15 Eagle.

The ATF was conceived in the first year of President Reagan's administration. In June 1981, a specification was issued whilst the F-15 and F-16 were quite new. At the time, however, there was a shortage of low-level, all-weather strike and interdiction aircraft. The Air Force set certain requirements and limits for the project. These subsequently included the ability to fly at supersonic speed without afterburner (known as supercruise), have enough fuel for mission radius, have unrestricted manoeuvrability with the use of two-dimensional engine nozzles, incorporate stealth technology and other systems to provide high survivability, internal weapons carriage in air-superiority role, conform to specific weight and cost requirements, have a cruise speed of Mach 1.5 with a combat radius of 800 miles, and more.

Two prototypes were ordered, one powered by Pratt & Whitney F119 engines, the other with General Electric F-120s. Boeing would build the wings and aft fuselage, General Dynamics the centre fuselage and empennage and Lockheed the cockpit and nose section.

Boeing provided a 757 for flight testing the complete avionics system, the first with active matrix liquid crystal displays instead of cathode ray tubes.

In 1987 radical redesign was undertaken because of weight problems; consequently, the contract was extended by six months.

The first YF-22 flew on 29 September 1990 and in 1991 the F-22/F119 engine combination was selected over the rival Northrop/McDonnell Douglas YF-23. A further 9 test aircraft (EMDs) followed, the first flying in September 1997, and it is expected that the USAF will receive 339 F-22As, with deliveries from the year 2002.

LOCKHEED MARTIN F-22A
Role: Advanced Tactical Fighter (ATF)
Crew/Accommodation: One (in 360° tear-drop pressurized cockpit)
Power Plant: Two 15,875 kgp (35,000 lb s.t.) Pratt & Whitney F119-PW-100 turbofans with reheat
Dimensions: Span 13.56 m (44.5 ft); length 18.92 m (62.08 ft); wing area 78.04 m² (840 sq ft)
Weights: Empty 14,515 kg (32,000 lb); MTOW 24,950 kg (55,000 lb)
Performance: Maximum speed Mach 2+, also quoted as Mach 1.8+; Mach 1.58 supercruise, also quoted as Mach 1.4+; operational ceiling 15,240 m (50,000 ft+); range 3,200 km+ (2,000 miles+)
Load: One M61A-2 20-mm cannon; two side bays with AIM-9M Sidewinder air-to-air missiles (one in each) and one main bay with up to six AIM-120C AMRAAM air-to-air missiles. 8 AMRAAMs can be carried under the wings. Attack weapons can be carried in main bay

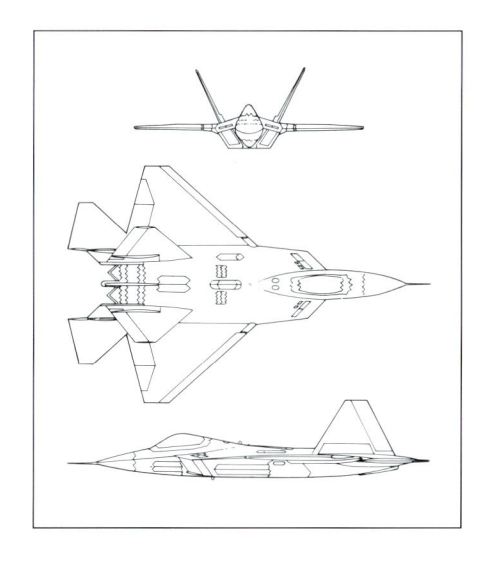

Lockheed Martin YF-22A Raptor

Heavy Bombers

Strategic bombing began at the very start of World War I, when in November 1914 three tiny Avro 504 biplanes of the Royal Naval Air Service set out to destroy the German Zeppelin sheds at Friedrichshafen. Each aircraft carried just four 20 lb bombs but still managed to damage Zeppelin LZ32 and blow up the adjacent gasworks.

Such tiny aircraft could hardly be termed strategic bombers, despite the nature of their historic mission, but in February 1915 giant four-engined Russian Sikorsky Ilya Mourometzs began their wartime raids with an attack on a target in Poland. It fell to Italy to begin the first sustained strategic bombing offensive when, from August 1915, triple-engined Caproni Ca 32s and other types began striking targets in Austria-Hungary. Ca 32s also recorded the first Italian night bombing raids.

Already, by January 1915, German Navy Zeppelin airships had begun bombing attacks on Great Britain, with London hit for the first time that May. Such attacks lasted until April 1918, the 51 Zeppelin raids on Britain dropping 199 tonnes of bombs and causing 557 fatalities. However, from 1917 Germany put greater faith in new Gotha and other heavy bombing aeroplanes to undertake strategic attacks, with the first mass raid by 21 Gothas recorded on 25 May. Despite some earlier success in bringing down Zeppelins, the British RFC and RNAS found the bombers a different matter and on that first raid no contacts with the enemy were made during 77 defence sorties. Night attacks by Gothas started in September 1917, the same month that Germany introduced even larger Zeppelin Staaken R VI bombers capable of dropping 1,000 kg bombs, the largest of the war.

In retaliation for German bombing of civilians, and to meet public outcry, in 1916 Britain fielded the Handley Page O/100, a twin-engined heavy bomber built to the Admiralty's call for a 'bloody paralyser'. It was followed by the high-powered O/400, but other heavy bombers such as the Vickers Vimy had hardly reached service status by the Armistice and so saw most service post-war. Indeed, the Vimy will always be remembered in the annals of aviation for carrying Alcock and Brown on the first-ever non-stop flight across the Atlantic in 1919.

The heavy bomber was, by the start of the 1920s, standard equipment for all major air forces and by the 1930s huge monoplanes began the slow process of superseding biplanes, with the Soviet Union establishing the world's most potent heavy bomber force with its Tupolev TB series of metal low-wing monoplanes. The stage was set for the development of the bombers used in World War II, as detailed in the following pages.

Picture: Zeppelin Staaken R VI represented Germany's largest bomber of World War I, some versions having six engines.

BOEING B-17 FLYING FORTRESS (U.S.A.)

B-17G Flying Fortress

The Flying Fortress was one of the United States' most important warplanes of World War II, and resulted from a 1934 requirement for a multi-engined bomber with the ability to carry a 907-kg (2,000-lb) bomb load over minimum and maximum ranges of 1640 and 3540 km (1,020 and 2,200 miles) at speeds between 322 and 402 km/h (200 and 250 mph). Boeing began work on its Model 299 design in June 1934, and the prototype flew in July 1935 with four 599-kW (750-hp) Pratt & Whitney R-1680-E Radials.

Although it crashed during a take-off in October 1935 as a result of locked controls, the prototype had demonstrated sufficiently impressive performance for the U.S. Army Air Corps to order 14 YB-17 (later Y1B-17) pre-production aircraft including the static test airframe brought up to flight standard. Twelve of these aircraft were powered by 694-kW (930-hp) Wright GR-1820-39 radials, while the thirteenth was completed as the Y1B-17A with 746-kW (1,000-hp) GR-1820-51 radials, each fitted with a turbocharger for improved high-altitude performance. The early production models were development variants and included 39 B-17Bs, 38 B-17Cs with 895-kW (1,200-hp) R-1820-65 engines, and 42 B-17Ds with self-sealing tanks and better armour. The tail was redesigned with a large dorsal fillet, which led to the first of the definitive Fortresses, the B-17E and B-17F, of which 512 and 3,405 were built, the latter with improved defensive armament.

The ultimate bomber variant was the B-17G with a chin turret and improved turbochargers for better ceiling, and this accounted for 8,680 of the 12,731 Flying Fortresses built. The type was discarded almost immediately after World War II, only a few special-purpose variants remaining in service. In addition, there were a number of experimental and navy models.

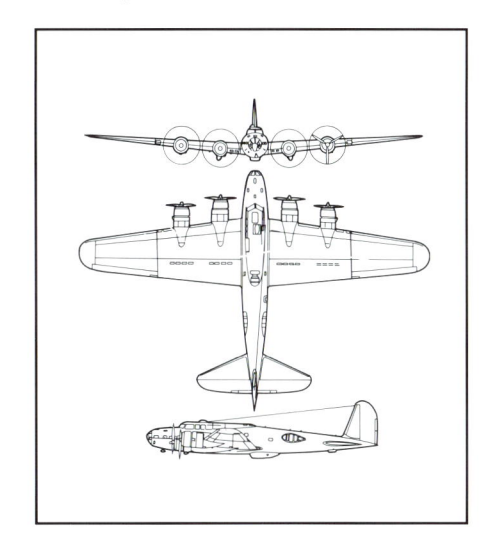

The definitive B-17G version of the Boeing B-17 Flying Fortress

BOEING B-17G FLYING FORTRESS
Role: Long-range day bomber
Crew/Accommodation: Ten
Power Plant: Four 1,200 hp Wright R-1820-97 Cyclone air-cooled radials
Dimensions: Span 31.62 m (103.75 ft); length 22.66 m (74.33 ft); wing area 131.92 m² (1,420 sq ft)
Weights: Empty 16,391 kg (36,135 lb); MTOW 29,484 kg (65,000 lb)
Performance: Maximum speed 462 km/h (287 mph) at 7,620 m (25,000 ft); operational ceiling 10,851 m (35,600 ft); range 5,472 km (3,400 miles)
Load: Twelve .5-inch machine guns, plus up to 2,722 kg (6,000 lb) of bombs

B-17C Flying Fortress

CONSOLIDATED B-24 LIBERATOR (U.S.A.)

B-24H Liberator

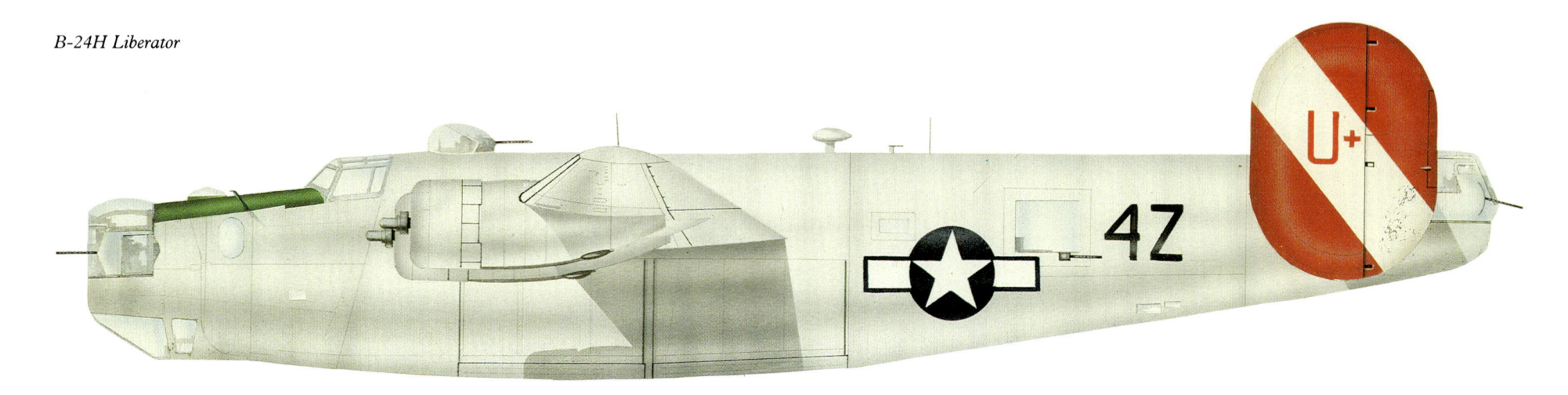

Consolidated B-24D Liberator

The Liberator was a remarkably versatile aircraft, and was built in greater numbers than any other U.S. warplane of World War II. The Model 32 was designed to a U.S. Army Air Corps request of January 1939 for a successor to machines such as the Boeing XB-15 and Douglas XB-19, neither of which entered production, and offering higher performance than the Boeing B-17.

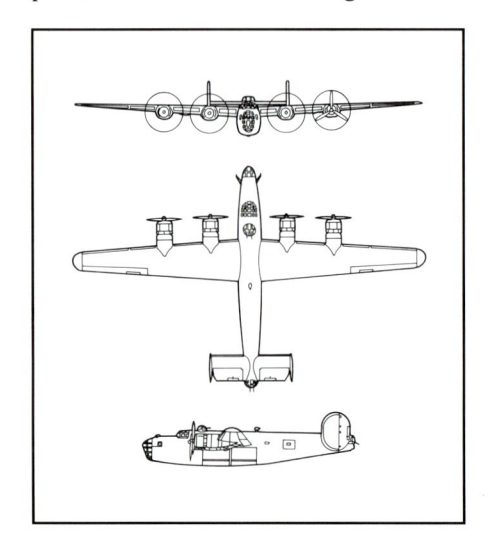

The design was based on the exceptional wing of the Model 31 flying boat, the high aspect ratio of which offered low drag and thus the possibility of high speed and great range. The XB-24 prototype flew in December 1939 with 895-kW (1,200-hp) R-1830-33 radial engines, and the seven YB-24 pre-production machines were followed by nine B-24As with two 7.62-mm (0.3-in) tail guns and six 12.7-mm (0.5-in) guns in nose, ventral, dorsal and waist positions, and nine B-24Cs with turbocharged R-1830-41 engines and eight 12.7-mm guns in single-gun nose, ventral, and twin waist positions, and twin-gun dorsal and tail turrets. These paved the way for the first major model, the B-24D based on the B-24C but with R-1830-43 engines, self-sealing tanks and, in later aircraft, a ventral ball turret together with two 12.7-mm guns.

These 2,381 aircraft were followed by 801 B-24Es with modified propellers. Then came 430 B-24Gs with R-1830-43 engines and a power-operated nose turret carrying twin 12.7-mm guns, and 3,100 improved B-24Hs with a longer nose. The most important variant was the slightly modified B-24J, of which 6,678 were built with R-1830-65 engines, an autopilot and an improved bombsight. The 1,667 B-24Ls were similar to the B-24Js but had hand-operated tail guns, as did the 2,593 B-24Ms in a lighter mounting. There were also a number of experimental bomber variants, while other roles included transport (LB-30, air force C-87 and navy RY variants), fuel tanking (C-109), photographic reconnaissance (F-7), patrol bombing (PB4Y-1 and specially developed PB4Y-2 with a single vertical tail surface) and maritime reconnaissance (British Liberator GR models).

CONSOLIDATED B-24J LIBERATOR
Role: Long-range day bomber
Crew/Accommodation: Ten
Power Plant: Four 1,200 hp Pratt & Whitney R.1830-65 Twin Wasp air-cooled radials
Dimensions: Span 33.53 m (110 ft); length 20.47 m (67.16 ft); wing area 97.36 m² (1,048 sq ft)
Weights: Empty 16,556 kg (36,500 lb); MTOW 29,484 kg (65,000 lb)
Performance: Maximum speed 467 km/h (290 mph) at 7,620 m (25,000 ft); operational ceiling 8,534 m (28,000 ft); range 3,379 km (2,100 miles) with full bombload
Load: Ten .5 inch machine guns, plus up to 3,992 kg (8,800 lb) of internally carried bombs

A Consolidated B-24D Liberator in USAAF markings

HANDLEY PAGE HALIFAX (United Kingdom)

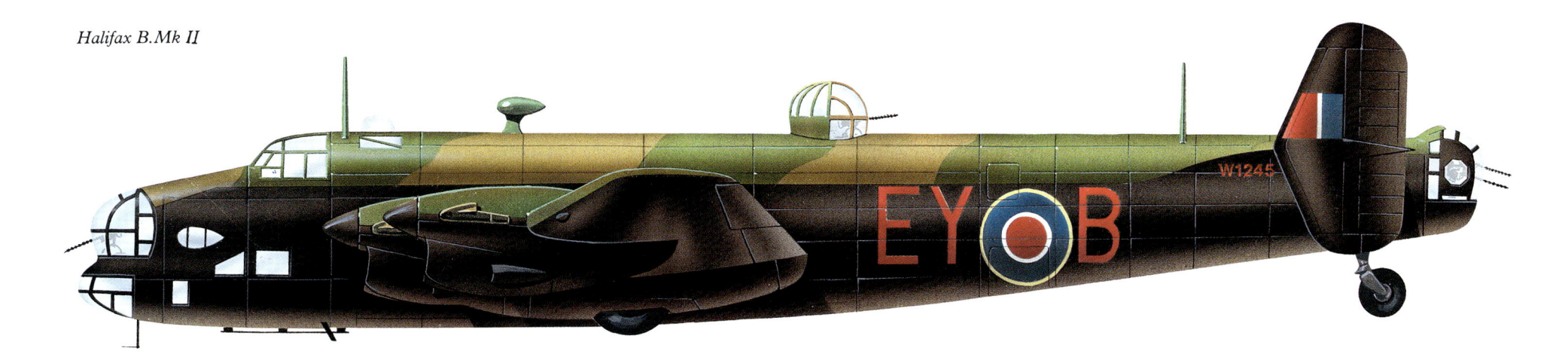

Halifax B.Mk II

The Halifax was one of the RAF's trio of four-engined night bombers in World War II, and while not as important in this role as the Lancaster, it was more important in secondary roles such as maritime reconnaissance, transport, and airborne forces' support. The type originated from a 1936 requirement for a medium/heavy bomber powered by two Rolls-Royce Vulture inline engines, and the resulting H.P.56 design was ordered in prototype form. The company had doubts about the Vulture, and began to plan an alternative H.P.57 with four Rolls-Royce Merlin inlines. In September 1937, two H.P.57 prototypes were ordered. The first flew in October 1939.

The type entered service as the Halifax B.Mk I with 954-kW (1,280-hp) Merlin Xs, and these 84 aircraft were produced in three series as the initial Series I, the higher-weight Series II, and the increased-tankage Series III. Later bombers were the 1,977 Halifax B.Mk IIs with Merlin XXs or 22s and a two-gun dorsal turret, the 2,091 Halifax B.Mk IIIs with 1204-kW (1,615-hp) Bristol Hercules VI or XVI radials, the 904 Halifax B.Mk Vs based on the Mk II with revised landing gear, the 467 Halifax B.Mk VIs based on the Mk III but with 1249-kW (1,675-hp) Hercules 100s, and the 35 Halifax B.Mk VIIs that reverted to Hercules XVIs; there were also bomber subvariants with important modifications. The other variants retained the same mark number as the relevant bomber variant, and in the transport type these were the C.Mks II, VI and VII, in the maritime role GR.Mks II, V and VI, and in the airborne support role the A.Mks II, V and VII. Post-war development produced the C.Mk 8 and A.Mk 9 as well as the Halton civil transport, and total production was 6,178 aircraft.

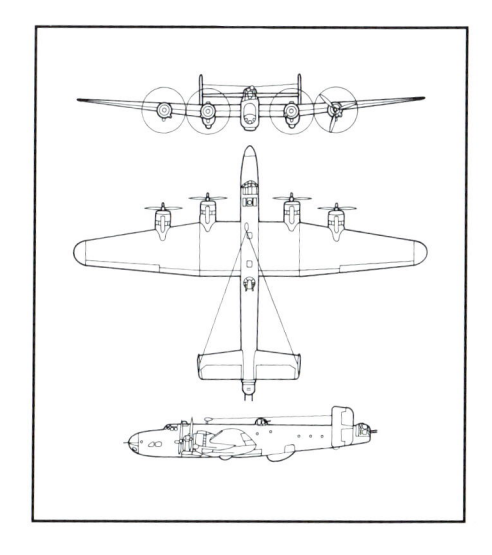

HANDLEY PAGE HALIFAX B.Mk III
Role: Heavy night bomber
Crew/Accommodation: Seven
Power Plant: Four 1,615 hp Bristol Hercules XVI air-cooled radials
Dimensions: Span 30.12 m (98.83 ft); length 21.82 m (71.58 ft); wing area 116.3 m² (1,250 sq ft)
Weights: Empty 17,346 kg (38,240 lb); MTOW 29,484 kg (65,000 lb)
Performance: Maximum speed 454 km/h (282 mph) at 4,115 m (13,500 ft); operational ceiling 7,315 m (24,000 ft); range 2,030 km (1,260 miles) with full warload
Load: Nine .303 inch machine guns, plus up to 5,897 kg (13,000 lb) of internally-stowed bombload

Handley Page Halifax Mk I

Handley Page Halifax B.Mk III

AVRO LANCASTER (United Kingdom)

Lancaster B.Mk III

Certainly the best night bomber of World War II, the Lancaster was conceived as a four-engined development of the twin-engined Type 679 Manchester, which failed because of the unreliability of its Rolls-Royce Vulture engines. The first Lancaster flew in January 1941 with 854-kW (1,145-hp) Rolls-Royce Merlin Xs and the same triple vertical tail surfaces as the Manchester, though these were later replaced by the larger endplate surfaces that became a Lancaster hallmark. The type was ordered into large-scale production as the Lancaster Mk I (later B.Mk I), of which 3,435 were produced. Defensive armament was eight 7.7-mm (0.303-in) machine-guns in three powered turrets: twin-gun nose and dorsal units, and a four-gun tail unit.

The first aircraft had 954-kW (1,280-hp) Merlin XXs or XXIIs, but later machines used the 1208-kW (1,620-hp) Merlin XXIVs. A feared shortage of Merlin inline engines led to the development of the Lancaster Mk II with 1294-kW (1,735-hp) Bristol Hercules VI or XVI radial engines, but only 301 of this model were built as performance was degraded and Merlins were in abundant supply. The Lancaster Mk I was soon supplemented by the Lancaster B.Mk III and Canadian-built Lancaster B.Mk X, both powered by Packard-built Merlins. Production of the Mk III and Mk X totalled 3,039 and 430 respectively. The final production version was the Lancaster B.Mk VIII with an American dorsal turret containing two 12.7-mm (0.5-in) heavy machine guns, and deliveries totalled 180 bringing overall Lancaster production to 7,377. After the war Lancasters were modified to perform a number of other roles.

AVRO LANCASTER Mk I
Role: Heavy night bomber
Crew/Accommodation: Seven
Power Plant: Four 1,640 hp Rolls-Royce Merlin 24 water-cooled inlines
Dimensions: Span 31.09 m (102 ft); length 21.18 m (69.5 ft); wing area 120.49 m² (1,297 sq ft)
Weights: Empty 16,780 kg (37,000 lb); MTOW 29,408 kg (65,000 lb)
Performance: Maximum speed 394 km/h (245 mph) at sea level; operational ceiling 6,706 m (22,000 ft); range 3,589 km (2,230 miles) with 3,182 kg (7,000 lb) bombload
Load: Eight .303 inch machine guns, plus up to 8,165 kg (18,000 lb) of bombs

Avro Lancaster Mk I

This is the RAF's preserved Avro Lancaster B.Mk I

HEAVY BOMBERS

BOEING B-29 and B-50 SUPERFORTRESS (U.S.A.)

B-29A Superfortress

B-29 Superfortress heavy bomber

The B-29 was the world's first genuinely effective long-range strategic bomber, and was designed from January 1940 as the Model 345 to meet the U.S. Army Air Corps' extremely ambitious plan for a 'hemisphere defense' bomber. The type was an extremely advanced design with pressurized accommodation, remotely controlled defensive armament, a formidable offensive load, and very high performance including great ceiling and range. The first of three XB-29 prototypes flew in September 1942 with four Wright R-3550 twin-row radials; each fitted with two turbochargers. By this time, Boeing already had contracts for more than 1,500 production bombers. The XB-29s were followed by 14 YB-29 pre-production aircraft, of which the first flew in June 1943.

A prodigious effort was made to bring the Superfortress into full service, and a wide-ranging programme of subcontracting delivered components to four assembly plants. The type entered full service in time to make a major contribution to the war against Japan in World War II, which it ended with the A-bombings of Hiroshima and Nagasaki in August 1945.

Some 2,848 B-29s were complemented by 1,122 B-29As with slightly greater span and revised defensive armament, and by 311 B-29Bs with no defensive armament but a radar-directed tail barbette. The type was also developed for reconnaissance and experimental roles, and was then revised with a sturdier structure and Pratt & Whitney R-4360 engines as the B-29D, which entered production as the B-50A. This was followed by its own series of bomber, reconnaissance and tanker aircraft.

BOEING B-29A SUPERFORTRESS
Role: Long-range, high altitude day bomber
Crew/Accommodation: Ten
Power Plant: Four 2,200 hp Wright R-3350-23 Cyclone Eighteen air-cooled radials
Dimensions: Span 43.05 m (141.25 ft); length 30.18 m (99 ft); wing area 161.56 m² (1,739 sq ft)
Weights: Empty 32,369 kg (71,360 lb); MTOW 62,823 kg (138,500 lb)
Performance: Maximum speed 576 km/h (358 mph) at 7,620 m (25,000 ft); operational ceiling 9,708 m (31,850 ft); range 6,598 km (4,100 miles) with 7,258 kg (16,000 lb) bombload
Load: One 20 mm cannon and twelve .5 inch machine guns, plus up to 9,072 kg (20,000 lb) of bombs

Boeing B-29 Superfortress

CONVAIR B-36 'PEACEMAKER' (U.S.A.)

B-36A 'Peacemaker'

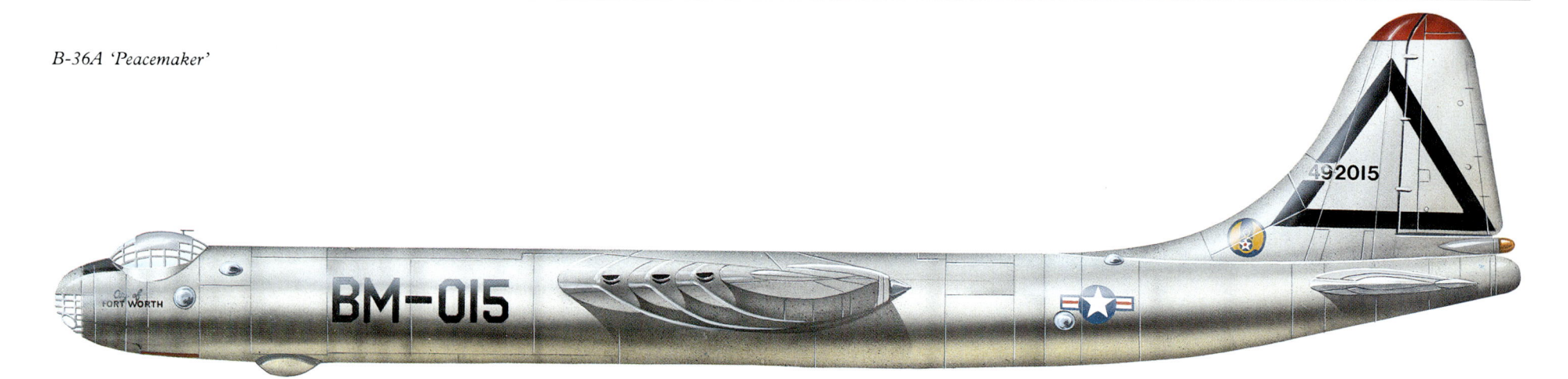

Designed as the Model 36 while the company was still Consolidated but built after it had become Convair, this extraordinary machine was the world's first genuinely intercontinental strategic bomber. The type resulted from an April 1941 requirement of the U.S. Army Air Corps for a machine able to carry a maximum bomb load of 32,659 kg (72,000 lb) but more realistically to deliver 4536 kg (10,000 lb) of bombs on European targets from bases in the United States. From four competing designs, the Model 36 was selected by the U.S. Army Air Forces for construction as the XB-36 prototype. This first flew in August 1946 and featured a pressurized fuselage and pusher propellers on the six 2237-kW (3,000-hp) R-4360-25 radial engines buried in the trailing edges of wings sufficiently deep to afford inflight access to the engines. The service trials model was the YB-36 with a raised cockpit roof, and this was subsequently modified as the YB-36A with four- rather than single-wheel main landing gear units. These were features of the first production model, the B-36A unarmed crew trainer of which 22 were built without armament. The 104 B-36Bs introduced 2610-kW (3,500-hp) R-4360-41 engines and a defensive armament of 16 20-mm cannon in nose, tail and six fuselage barbettes. Some 64 were later revised as B-36D strategic reconnaissance aircraft with greater weights and performance through the addition of four 2359-kg (5,200-lb) thrust General Electric J47-GE-19 turbojets in podded pairs under the outer wing, and in this role they complemented 22 aircraft which were built as such.

Later bombers with greater power and improved electronics were the 34 B-36Fs with 2833-kW (3,800-hp) R-04360-53s and J47-GE-19s, 83 B-36Hs with an improved flight deck, and 33 B-36Js with strengthened landing gear. There were also RB-36D, E, F and H reconnaissance versions, and even the GRB-36F with an embarked fighter for protection over the target area. Plans for jet- and even nuclear-powered versions resulted in no production variants.

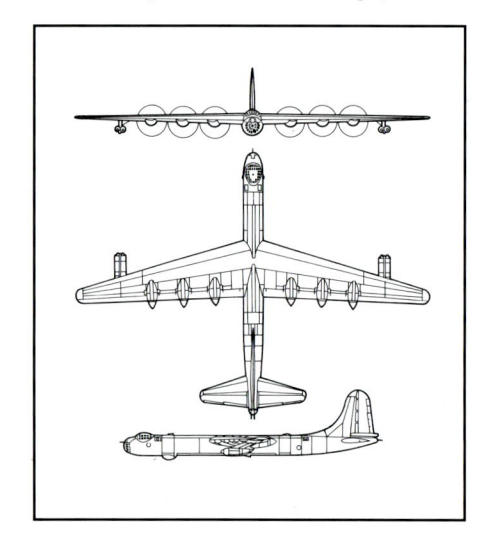

CONSOLIDATED/CONVAIR B-36D
Role: Long-range heavy bomber
Crew/Accommodation: Fifteen, including four relief crew members
Power Plant: Six 3,500 hp Pratt & Whitney R-4360-41 air-cooled radials, plus four 2,359 kgp (5,200 lb s.t.) General Electric J47-GE-19 turbojets
Dimensions: Span 70.1 m (230 ft); length 49.4 m (162.08 ft); wing area 443 m² (4,772 sq ft)
Weights: Empty 72,051 kg (158,843 lb); MTOW 162,161 kg (357,500 lb)
Performance: Maximum speed 706 km/h (439 mph) at 9,790 m (32,120 ft); operational ceiling 13,777 m (45,200 ft); range 12,070 km (7,500 miles) with 4,535 kg (10,000 lb bombload)
Load: Twelve 20 mm cannon, plus up to 39,009 kg (86,000 lb) of bombs

Convair B-36H

A Convair B-36B in its original form

BOEING B-47 STRATOJET (U.S.A.)

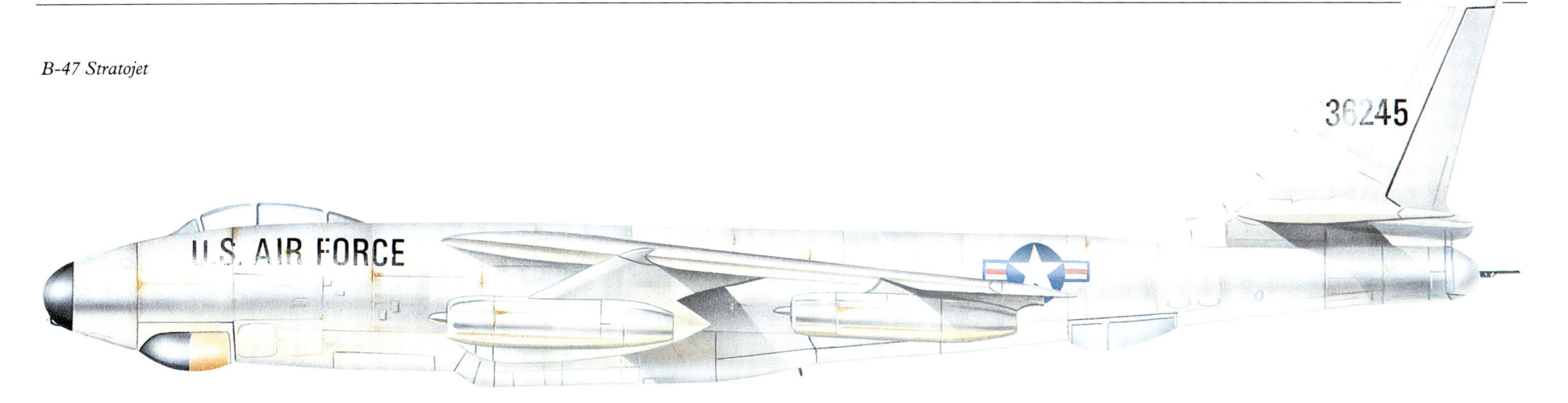

B-47 Stratojet

The B-47 was a great achievement, and as a swept-wing strategic bomber in the medium-range bracket it formed the main strength of the U.S. Strategic Air Command in the early 1950s. The U.S. Army Air Forces first considered a jet-powered bomber as early as 1944; at that time four companies were involved in producing preliminary designs for such a type. The Model 424 failed to attract real interest, but the later Model 432 was thought more acceptable and initial contracts were let. The company then recast the design as the Model 448 with the swept flying surfaces that captured German research data had shown to be desirable, but the USAAF was unimpressed. The design was finalized as the Model 450 with the six engines relocated from the fuselage to two twin-unit and two single-unit underwing nacelles.

In the spring of 1946, the USAAF ordered two Model 450 prototypes with the designation XB-47 and the first of these flew in December 1947. The type was notable for many of its features including the 'bicycle' type landing gear the twin main units of which retracted into the fuselage. The 10 B-47As were essentially development aircraft, and the first true service variant was the 399 B-47Bs, followed by 1,591 B-47Es with a host of operational improvements including greater power, inflight refuelling capability, and ejector seats. The B-47B and B-47E were both strengthened structurally later in their lives, leading to the designations B-47B-II and B-47E-II. There were also RB-47 reconnaissance together with several special-purpose and experimental variants.

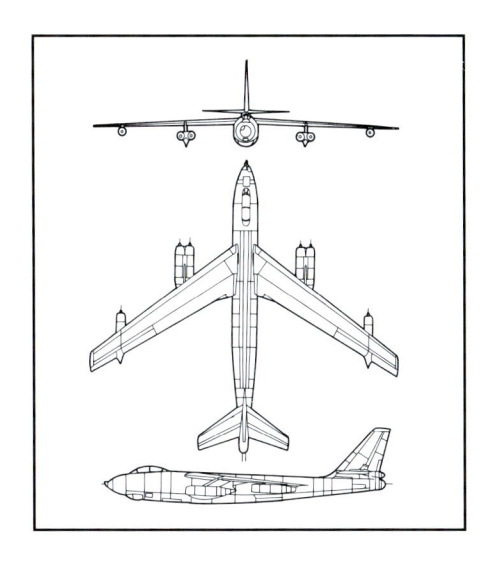

BOEING B-47E STRATOJET
Role: Heavy bomber
Crew/Accommodation: Three
Power Plant: Six 3,266 kgp (7,200 lb s.t.) General Electric J47-GE-25 turbojets, plus a 16,329 kgp (36,000 lb s.t.) rocket pack for Jet Assisted Take-Off (JATO)
Dimensions: Span 35.36 m (116 ft); length 32.92 m (108 ft); wing area 132.67 m² (1,428 sq ft)
Weights: Empty 36.631 kg (80,756 lb); MTOW 93,759 kg (206,700 lb) with JATO rocket assistance
Performance: Maximum speed 975 km/h (606 mph) at 4,968 m (16,300 ft); operational ceiling 12,344 m (40,500 ft); range 6,228 km (3,870 miles) with 4,536 kg (10,000 lb) bombload
Load: Two rear-firing 20 mm cannon, plus up to 9,979 kg (22,000 lb) of bombs

Boeing B-47E bomber

Boeing B-47E Stratojet

VICKERS VALIANT (UNITED KINGDOM)

Valiant B(K).Mk 1

The Valiant was the first of the U.K.'s trio of strategic V-bombers to enter service and, though not as advanced or capable as the later Avro Vulcan and Handley Page Victor, it was nonetheless a worthy warplane. The Type 667 was originated in response to a 1948 requirement for a high-altitude bomber to carry the British free-fall nuclear bomb that would be dropped with the aid of a radar bombing system. The type was based on modestly swept flying surfaces that included a shoulder-set cantilever wing with compound-sweep leading edges, a circular-section fuselage accommodating the five-man crew in its pressurized forward section, retractable tricycle landing gear, and, in addition, four turbojets buried in the wing roots.

The prototype first flew in May 1951 with 2948-kg (6,500-lb) Rolls-Royce Avon RA.3 turbojets, improved to 3402-kg (7,500-lb) thrust Avon RA.7s in the second prototype that took over the flight test programme after the first had been destroyed by fire. The first five of 36 Valiant B.Mk 1 bombers served as pre-production aircraft, and this type began to enter squadron service in 1955. The type was used operationally as a conventional bomber in the Suez campaign of 1956, and was also used to drop the first British atomic and hydrogen bombs in October 1956 and May 1957 respectively. Production for the RAF totalled 104 aircraft in the form of 36 Valiant B.Mk 1 bombers, 11 Valiant B(PR).Mk. 1 strategic reconnaissace aircraft, 13 Valiant B(PR).Mk 1 multi-role aircraft usable in the bomber, reconnaissance and inflight refuelling tanker tasks, and 44 Valiant B(K).Mk 1 bomber and tanker aircraft. The Valiant B.Mk 2 did not pass the prototype stage, and all surviving aircraft were retired in 1965 as a result of fatigue problems.

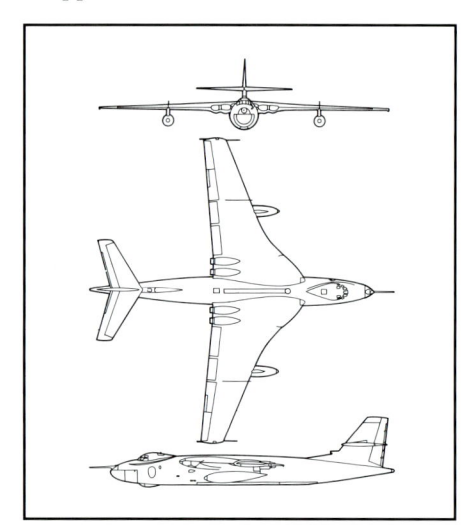

VICKERS VALIANT B.Mk 1
Role: Strategic bomber
Crew/Accommodation: Five
Power Plant: Four 4,536 kgp (10,000 lb s.t.) Rolls-Royce Avon 28 turbojets
Dimensions: Span 34.85 m (114.33 ft); length 32.99 m (108.25 ft); wing area 219.4 m² (2,362 sq ft)
Weights: Empty 34,419 kg (75,881 lb); MTOW 63,503 kg (140,000 lb)
Performance: Maximum speed 912 km/h (492 knots) at 9,144 m (30,000 ft); operational ceiling 16,459 m (54,000 ft); range 7,242 km (3,908 naut. miles) with maximum fuel
Load: No defensive armament, but internal stowage for up to 9,525 kg (21,000 lb) of bombs

Vickers Valiant B(K).Mk 1

Vickers Valiant B.Mk 1 bomber

BOEING B-52 STRATOFORTRESS (U.S.A.)

HEAVY BOMBERS

B-52G Stratofortress in early form

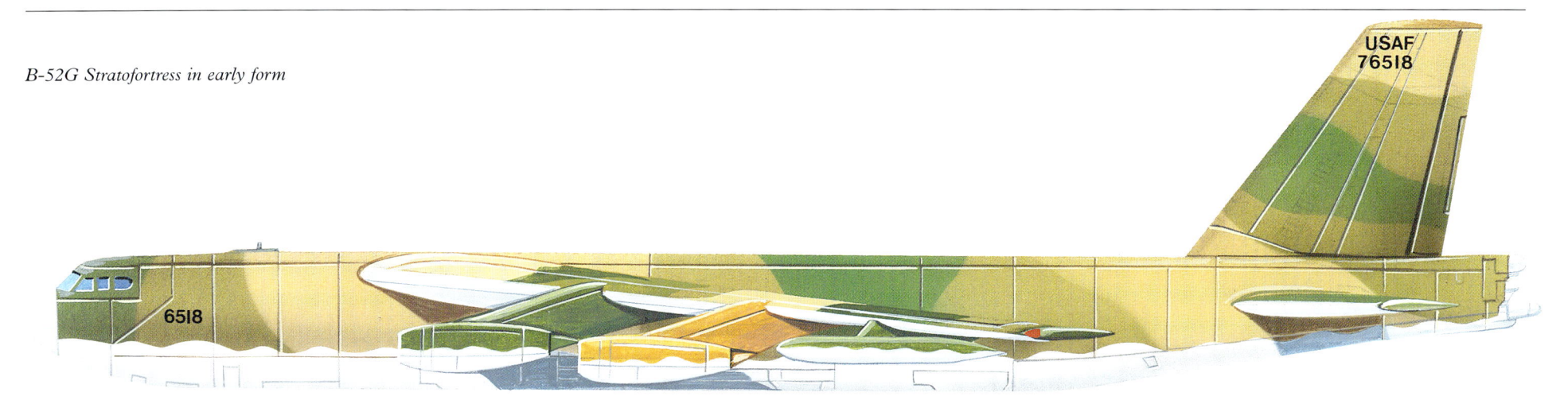

In numerical terms, the B-52 is still the most important bomber in the U.S. Strategic Air Command inventory. It offers an excellent combination of great range and very large payload, though the type's radar signature is large and its operational capabilities are ensured only by constantly updated offensive and defensive electronic systems.

The Stratofortress was first planned as a turboprop-powered successor to the B-50, but was then recast as a turbojet-powered type using eight 3402-kg (7,500-lb) thrust Pratt & Whitney J57s podded in four pairs under the swept wings. The B-52 employs the same type of 'bicycle' landing gear as the B-47, and after design as the Model 464 the XB-52 prototype first flew in April 1952 with a high-set cockpit that seated the two pilots in tandem. The current cockpit was adopted in the B-52A, of which three were built as development aircraft. The 50 B-52Bs introduced the standard nav/attack system, and the 35 B-52Cs had improved equipment and performance. These were in reality development models, and the first true service version was the B-52D, of which 170 were built with revised tail armament. This model was followed by 100 B-52Es with improved navigation and weapon systems, 89 B-52Fs with greater power, 193 B-52Gs with a shorter fin, remotely controlled tail armament, integral fuel tankage and underwing pylons for two AGM-28 Hound Dog stand-off nuclear missiles, and 102 B-52Hs, with Pratt & Whitney TF33 turbofans, a rotary-barrel cannon as tail armament, and structural strengthening for the low-altitude role.

The only version currently in service is the B-52H, capable of carrying more than a 22,680-kg (50,000-lb) load. Apart from conventional weapons such as bombs, B-52H has an anti-shipping capability using Harpoon missiles, while for a nuclear mission it can carry up to twenty air-launched cruise missiles or a mix of these and gravity bombs. Other new missiles are also coming on stream for B-52H.

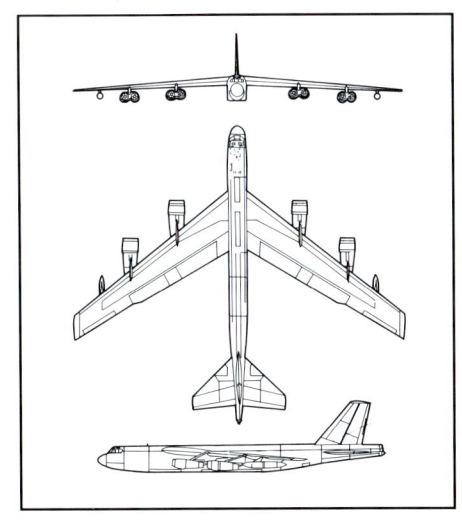

BOEING B-52H STRATOFORTRESS
Role: Long-range bomber
Crew/Accommodation: Six
Power Plant: Eight 7,718 kgp (17,000 lb s.t.) Pratt & Whitney TF33-P-3 turbofans.
Dimensions: Span 56.42 m (185 ft); length 49.04 m (160 ft); wing area 371.6 m² (4,000 sq ft)
Weights: Empty 78,355 kg (172,740 lb); MTOW 221,350 kg (488,000 lb)
Performance: Maximum speed 958 km/h (595 mph) at high altitude; operational ceiling 16,750 m (55,000 ft); range 16,090 km (10,000 miles)
Load: More than 22,680 kg (50,000 lb) of bombs or missiles

A Boeing B-52G Stratofortress

AVRO VULCAN (United Kingdom)

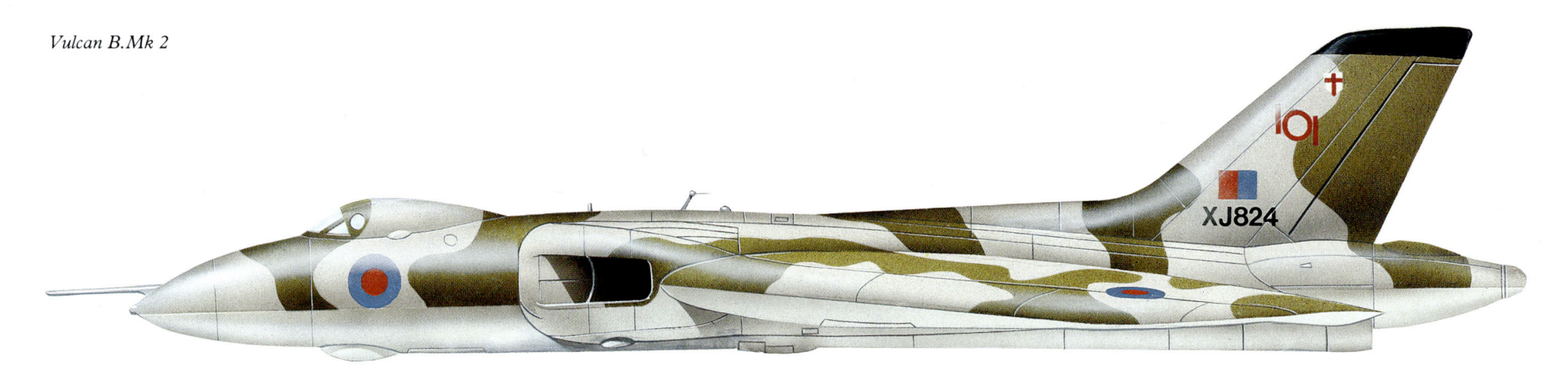

Vulcan B.Mk 2

The Type 698 was a massively impressive delta-winged bomber, and by any standards was an extraordinary aerodynamic feat that, with the Handley Page Victor and Vickers Valiant, was one of the U.K.'s trio of nuclear 'V-bombers' from the 1950s. The type was planned as a high-altitude bomber able to deliver the British free-fall nuclear bomb over long ranges. The first of two Type 698 prototypes flew in August 1952 with four 2,948-kg (6,500-lb) thrust Rolls-Royce Avon RA.3 turbojets, later replaced by 3,629-kg (8,000-lb) thrust Armstrong Siddeley Sapphire turbojets. The initial production model, the Vulcan B.Mk 1, had Olympus turbojet in variants increased in thrust from 4,990 to 6,123-kg (11,000 to 13,500-lb).

In 1961 existing aircraft were modified to Vulcan B.Mk 1A standard with a bulged tail containing electronic counter-measures gear. The definitive model was the Vulcan B.Mk 2 with provision for the Avro Blue Steel stand-off nuclear missile, a turbofan powerplant offering considerably greater fuel economy as well as more power, and a much-modified wing characterized by a cranked leading edge and offering greater area as well as elevons in place of the Mk 1's separated elevators and ailerons. The type was later modified as the Vulcan B.Mk 2A for the low-level role with conventional bombs and ECM equipment, and the Vulcan SR.Mk 2 was a strategic reconnaissance derivative.

Soon after the outbreak of the 1982 Falklands War, an RAF Vulcan attacked Port Stanley airfield; the flight from its Ascension Island base was then the largest ever operational sortie. Final retirement followed soon after.

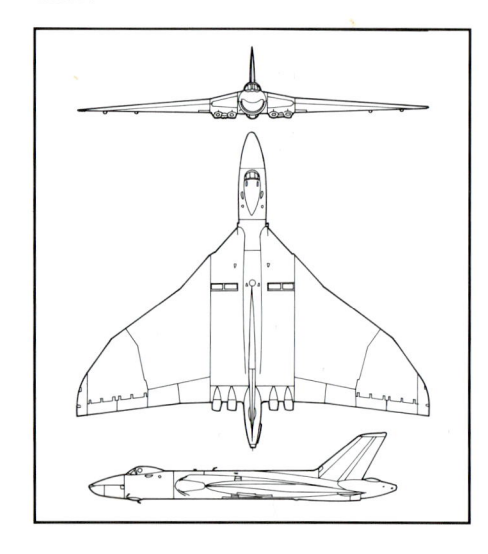

An Avro Vulcan B.Mk 2

AVRO VULCAN B.Mk 2
Role: Long-range bomber
Crew/Accommodation: Five
Power Plant: Four 9,072 kgp (20,000 lb s.t.) Bristol Siddeley Olympus 301 turbojets
Dimensions: Span 33.83 m (111 ft); length 30.45 m (99.92 ft); wing area 368.29 m² (3,964 sq ft)
Weights: Empty 48,081 kg (106,000 lb); MTOW 98,800 kg (200,180 lb)
Performance: Maximum speed 1,041 km/h (562 knots) Mach 0.98 at 12,192 m (40,000 ft); operational ceiling 19,912 m (65,000 ft); radius 3,701 km (2,300 miles) at altitude with missile
Load: Up to 9,525 kg (21,000 lb) of bombs, or one Blue Steel Mk 1 stand-off missile

Avro Vulcan B.Mk 2A

TUPOLEV Tu-95 and Tu-142 'BEAR' (U.S.S.R.)

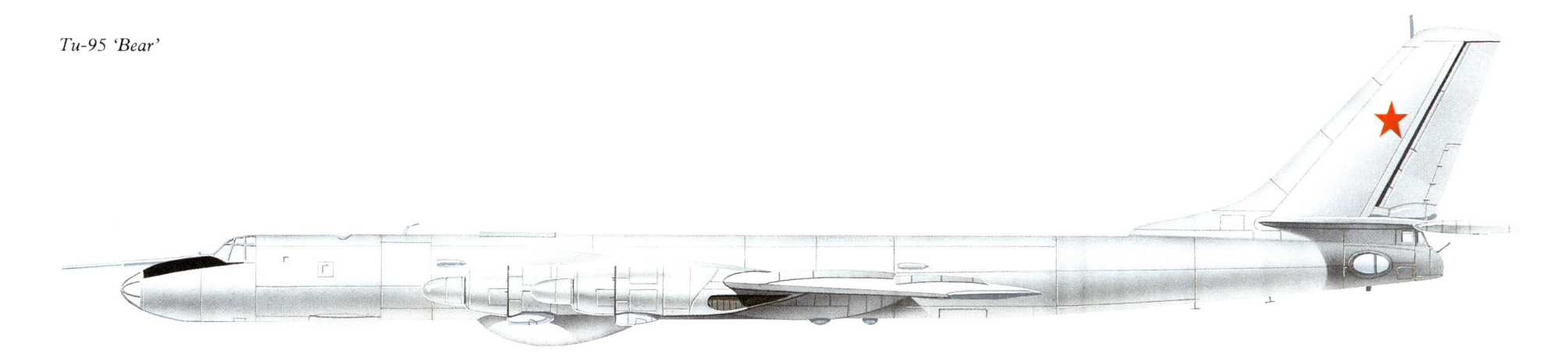

Tu-95 'Bear'

The Tu-95 prototype first flew in November 1952 and the type entered service in 1957. An extraordinary feature of this giant bomber was the adoption of massive turboprop engines, despite the official requirement for a speed of 900–950 km/h and a range of 14,000–15,000 km with a nuclear bomb. 'Bear-A' and 'Bear-B' were the original versions, the latter carrying the AS-3 'Kangaroo' missile semi-recessed under the fuselage, while retrofits later added inflight refuelling and, in some aircraft, strategic reconnaissance capabilities. Introduced in about 1963, the 'Bear-C' carried photographic and electronic reconnaissance equipment. 'Bear-D' appeared in 1962 as a multi-sensor maritime reconnaissance and sea target acquisition version for the Soviet navy. It was followed by 'Bear-E' for photographic reconnaissance and, from the mid-1970s, by 'Bear-G' to carry AS-4 'Kitchen' missiles but was also used for electronic intelligence. All of these versions are now out of service. The 'Bear-H' first flew in 1979 and remains operational, armed with AS-15 'Kent' cruise missiles.

The TU-142 designation was applied to a long-range anti-submarine version of the Tu-95 for the Soviet navy, first flown in 1968 and which remained in production until 1994. The ASW 'Bear-F' entered service in 1972 and remains operational with Russia and India. A communications relay variant became known to NATO as 'Bear-J' and continues in its role of providing an emergency link between the government and its nuclear submarines.

Tupolev Tu-95 'Bear-H'

TUPOLEV Tu142 'BEAR-F'
Role: Long-range anti-submarine warfare
Crew/Accommodation: Eleven to thirteen (mission dependent)
Power Plant: Four 15,000 eshp Kuznetsov NK-P 12M turboprops driving contra-rotating propellers
Dimensions: Span 50.04 m (164.17 ft); length 53.07 m (174.08 ft); wing area 289.9 m² (3,121 sq ft)
Weights: Empty 91,800 kg (202,384 lb); MTOW 185,000 kg (407,885 lb)
Performance: Maximum speed 855 km/h (531 mph); operational ceiling 11,000 m (36,000 ft); range 12,000 km (7,456 miles)
Load: Two 23-mm cannons and up to 9,000 kg (19,842 lb) of weaponry

A variant of the Tupolev Tu-95 family, a 'Bear-D'

HANDLEY PAGE VICTOR (United Kingdom)

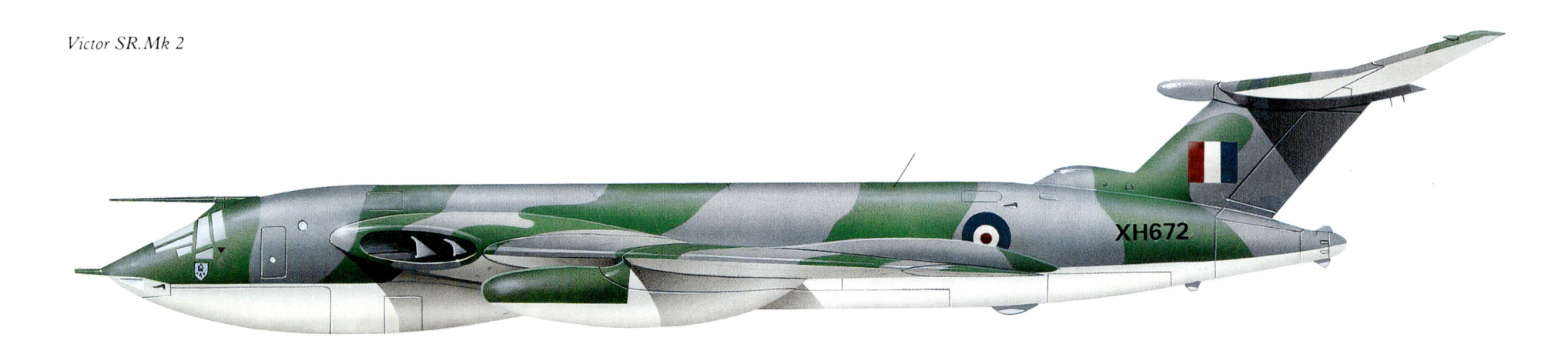

Victor SR.Mk 2

The last of the United Kingdom's trio of nuclear 'V-bombers' to enter service, it is now the only one still in service, albeit as a tanker. The type was planned against the requirements of a 1946 specification for a bomber able to carry a free-fall nuclear bomb over long range at a speed and altitude too high for interception by the fighters of the day. The H.P.80 was based on what was in effect a pod-and-boom fuselage that supported crescent-shaped flying surfaces. For its time it was a very advanced type. The first of two prototypes flew in December 1952.

After considerable development, the type entered squadron service in November 1957 with 5012-kg (11,050-lb) thrust Armstrong Siddeley Sapphire ASSa.7 Mk 202 turbojets. Production totalled just 50 aircraft that were formally designated Victor B.Mk 1H with better equipment and electronic counter-measures than the basic Victor B.Mk 1 that had originally been planned; soon after delivery, 24 aircraft were modified to Victor B.Mk 1A standard with improved defensive electronics. Though planned with Sapphire ASSa.9 engines in a wing increased in span to 34.05 m (115 ft 0 in), the radically improved Victor B.Mk 2 was delivered with Rolls-Royce Conway turbofans, initially 7824-kg (17,250-lb) thrust RCo.11 Mk 200s, but then in definitive form 9344-kg (20,600-lb) thrust Conway Mk 201s. Production totalled 34 aircraft, and of these 21 were modified to Victor B.Mk 2R standard with provision for the Avro Blue Steel stand-off nuclear missile that allowed the Victor to avoid flight over heavily defended targets. Soon after this, the Victor was retasked to the low-level role as Soviet defensive capability was thought to have made high-altitude overflights little more than suicidal. Later conversions were the nine Victor B(SR).Mk 2 maritime reconnaissance and the tanker models that included 11 Victor K.Mk 1s, six Victor B.Mk 1A(K2P)s, 14 Victor K.Mk 1As and 24 Victor K.Mk 2s.

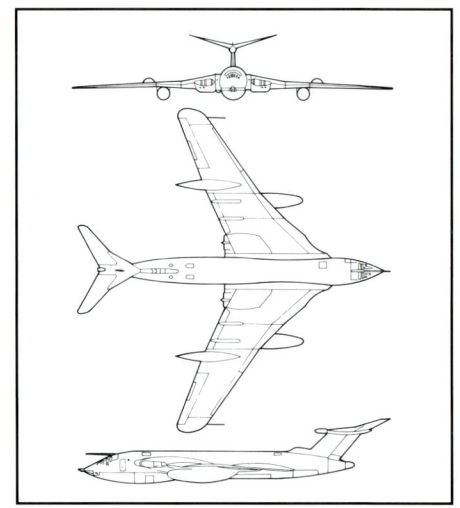

HANDLEY PAGE VICTOR K.Mk 2
Role: Air-to-air refueller
Crew/Accommodation: Five
Power Plant: Four 9,344 kgp (20,600 lb s.t.) Rolls-Royce Conway Mk.201 turbo fans
Dimensions: Span 35.69 m (117 ft); length 35.02 m (114.92 ft); wing area 204.38 m² (2,200 sq ft)
Weights: Empty 33,550 kg (110,000 lb); MTOW 101,150 kg (223,000 lb)
Performance: Maximum speed 1,020 km/h (550 knots) Mach 0.96 at 11,000 m (36,090 ft); operational ceiling 15,850 m (52,000 ft); range 7,403 km (3,995 naut. miles) unrefuelled
Load: Up to 15,876 kg (35,000 lb)

A Handley Page Victor B.Mk 2

Handley Page Victor B.Mk 2

CONVAIR B-58 HUSTLER (U.S.A.)

B-58A Hustler

The B-58 Hustler resulted from a 1949 U.S. Air Force requirement for a supersonic medium strategic bomber and was a stupendous technical achievement. In 1952 the Convair Model 4 was selected for development as an initial 18 aircraft. Convair's own experience in delta-winged aircraft, themselves based on German data captured at the end of World War II, was used in the far-sighted concept. The smallest possible airframe required advances in aerodynamics, structures, and materials, and was designed on Whitcomb area ruling principles with a long but slender fuselage that carried only a tall vertical tail and a small delta wing. This latter supported the nacelles for the four afterburning turbojets. The airframe was too small to accommodate sufficient fuel for both the outbound and return legs of the Hustler's mission, so the tricycle landing gear had very tall legs that raised the fuselage high enough off the ground to accommodate a large underfuselage pod 18.90 m (62 ft 0 in) long. This pod contained the Hustler's nuclear bombload and also the fuel for the outward leg, and was dropped over the target. The crew of three was seated in tandem escape capsules.

In July 1954 the order was reduced to two XB-58 prototypes, 11 YB-58A pre-production aircraft, and 31 pods. The first XB-58 flew in November 1956, and proved tricky to fly. Extensive development was undertaken with the aid of another 17 YB-58As ordered in February 1958 together with 35 pods; the last 17 YB-58As were later converted to RB-58A standard with ventral reconnaissance pods. The type became operational in 1960, but as the high-altitude bomber was clearly obsolescent, full production amounted to only 86 B-58As plus 10 upgraded YB-58As. Training was carried out in eight TB 58A conversions of YB-58As.

CONVAIR B-58A HUSTLER
Role: Supersonic bomber
Crew/Accommodation: Three
Power Plant: Four 7,076 kgp (15,600 lb s.t.) General Electric J79-GE-3B turbojets with reheat
Dimensions: Span 17.32 m (56.83 ft); length 29.49 m (96.75 ft); wing area 143.26 m² (1,542 sq ft)
Weights: Empty 25,202 kg (55,560 lb); MTOW 73,936 kg (163,000 lb)
Performance: Maximum speed 2,126 km/h (1,147 knots) Mach 2.1 at 12,192 m (40,000 ft); operational ceiling 19,202 m (63,000 ft); range 8,247 km (4,450 naut. miles) unrefuelled
Load: One 20 mm multi-barrel cannon, plus up to 8,820 kg (19,450 lb) of stores and fuel carrier in mission pod

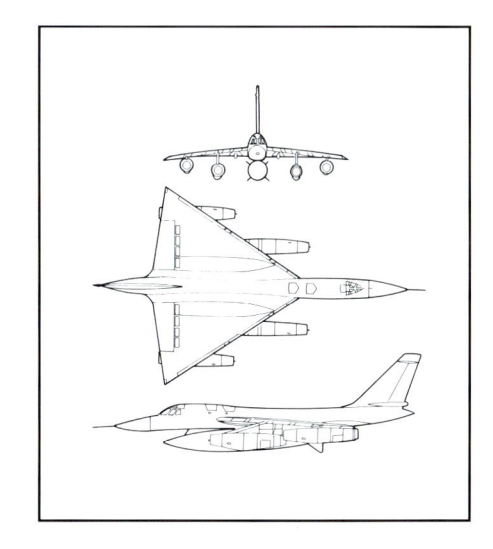

The Convair B-58A Hustler

Convair B-58A Hustler

ROCKWELL B-1B LANCER (U.S.A.)

B-1A

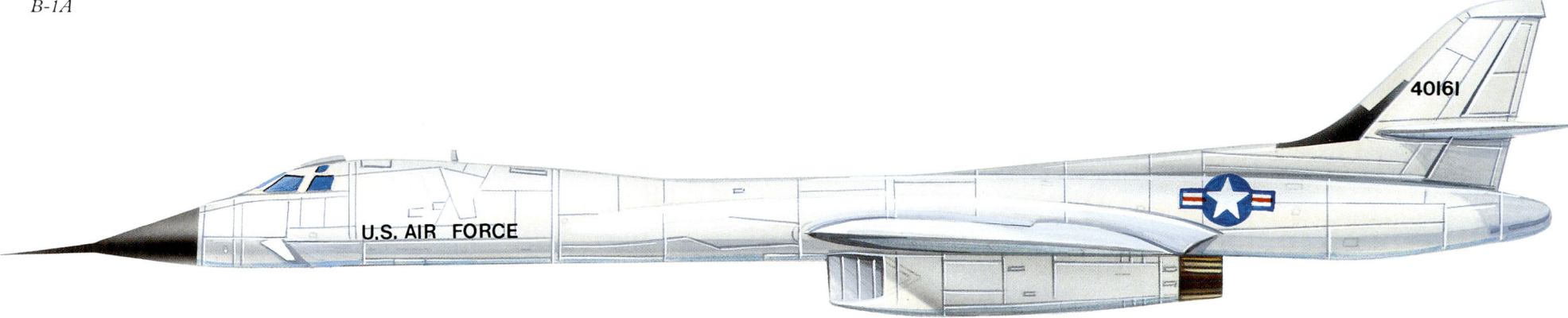

Entering service from July 1985 to supersede the Boeing B-52 in the penetration bomber role, the B-1B resulted from a protracted development history that began in 1965 when the U.S. Air Force issued a requirement for an Advanced Manned Strategic Bomber. This was expected to have a dash capability of Mach 2.2+ for delivery of free-fall and stand-off weapons. The U.S. Department of Defense issued a request for proposals in 1969 and the Rockwell submission was accepted as the B-1 in 1970, and the full-scale development was soon under way as a complex variable-geometry type with General Electric F101 turbofans and variable inlets.

The prototype first flew in December 1974 and the flight test programme moved ahead without undue delay. In June 1977, however, President Carter made the decision to scrap the programme in favour of cruise missiles, but the administration of President Reagan reactivated the programme in 1981 to procure just 100 B-1B bombers in the revised very low-level penetration role, using an automatic terrain following system. Other features included fixed inlets and modified nacelles (reducing speed to Mach 1.25) and a strengthened airframe and landing gear for operation at higher weights. Further changes were concerned with reduction of the type's already low radar signature, including some use of radar absorbent materials. The second and fourth B-1s were used from March 1983 to flight-test features of the B-1B, which itself first flew in October 1984 with the advanced offensive and defensive electronic systems. The second B-1B flew in May 1985 and became the first to join the Air Force, in July 1985. From the ninth aircraft the type was built with revised weapons bays, the forward bay having a movable bulkhead allowing the carriage of 12 AGM-86B ALCMs internally, as well as additional fuel tanks and SRAMs. The final B-1B was delivered in April 1988, and currently some 77 are in the active inventory. Since 1993 emphasis has also been placed on giving the B-1B a conventional weapon capability, though remaining a nuclear bomber. Upgrading for new weapons continues.

ROCKWELL B-1B
Role: Long-range low-level variable-geometry stand-off, strategic and conventional bomber
Crew/Accommodation: Four
Power Plant: Four 13,960 kpg (30,780 lb s.t.) General Electric F101-GE-102 turbofans with reheat
Dimensions: Span 41.66 m (136.68 ft); swept 23.84 m (78.23 ft); length 44.43 m (145.75 ft); wing area 181.2 m² (1,950 sq ft)
Weights: Empty 87,090 kg (192, 000 lb); MTOW 213,367 kg (477,000 lb)
Performance: Maximum speed 966 km/h (600 mph) at low level or Mach 1.2 at altitude; operational ceiling 15,240+ m (50,000+ ft); range 12,070 km (7,500 miles)
Load: Up to 56,699 kg (125,000 lb) of weapons as absolute maximum, including up to 24 nuclear bombs, 84 x 500 lb conventional bombs, sea mines, JDAM missiles or other weapons

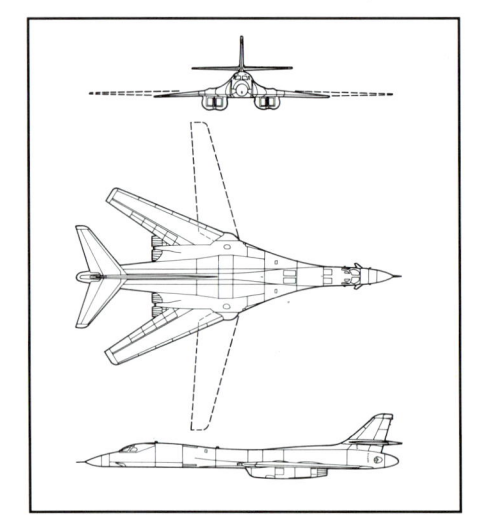

Rockwell B-1B

Rockwell B-1B Lancer

NORTHROP GRUMMAN B-2A SPIRIT (U.S.A.)

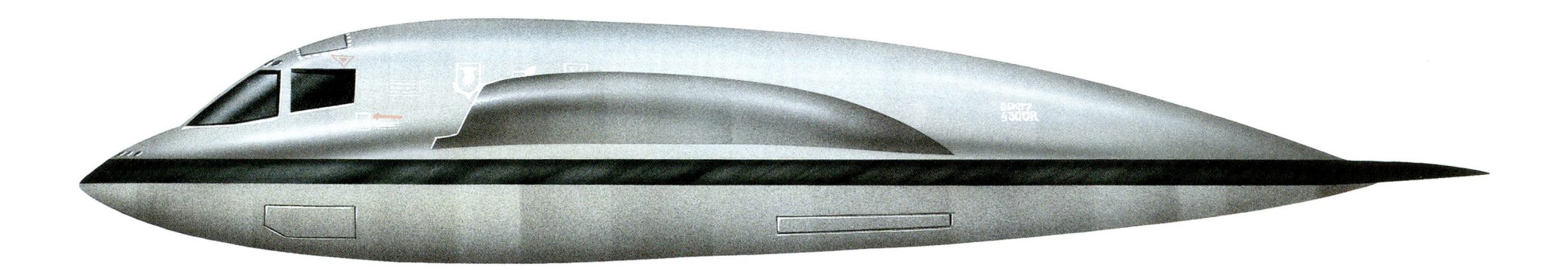

Developed at enormous cost during the late 1970s and 1980s, and first revealed in November 1988 for an initial flight in July 1989, the B-2 was designed as successor to the Rockwell B-1B in the penetration bomber role, although now intended to supplement it due partly to the tiny number built. Unlike the low-altitude B-1B, however, the B-2 is designed for penetration of enemy airspace at medium and high altitudes, relying on its stealth design, composite structure and defensive avionics suite to evade detection by an enemy until it has closed to within a few miles of its target, where attack accuracy is enhanced by use of the APQ-181 low-probability-of-intercept radar. Thereby, B-2A can strike at maximum defended and moving targets, allowing follow-up raids by non-stealth aircraft.

The B-2 is a design of the relaxed-stability type, and is a flying wing with highly swept leading edges and W-shaped trailing edges featuring all-horizontal flight-control surfaces (2-section elevons functioning as elevators and ailerons, and 2-section outer surfaces performing as drag rudders, spoilers and airbrakes) operated by a fly-by-wire control system. The design emphasis was placed on completely smooth surfaces with blended flightdeck and nacelle bulges. Radar reflectivity is very low because of the use of radiation-absorbent materials and a carefully optimized shape (including shielded upper-surface inlets), and the head-on radar cross-section is only about one-tenth of that of the B-1B.

Production of 132 B-2s was originally planned, but this total was progressively lowered until just 21 were completed for service, a figure including all six development aircraft raised to operational standard. The final B-2A was delivered in 1998 and full operational capability was achieved in 1999.

NORTHROP B-2A
Role: Long-range subsonic stealth bomber
Crew/Accommodation: Two/three
Power Plant: Four 8,620 kgp (19,000 lb s.t.) General Electric F118-GE-100 turbofans
Dimensions: Span 52.43 m (172 ft); length 21.03 m (69 ft); wing area about 477.5 m² (5,140 sq ft)
Weights: Empty 56,700 kg (125,000 lb); MTOW 170,550 kg (376,000 lb)
Performance: Maximum speed Mach 0.8; operational ceiling 15,240 m (50,000 ft); range 11,100 km (6,900 miles) with a 14,515 kg (32,000 lb) load.
Load: Up to 18,145 kg (40,000 lb) in two bays

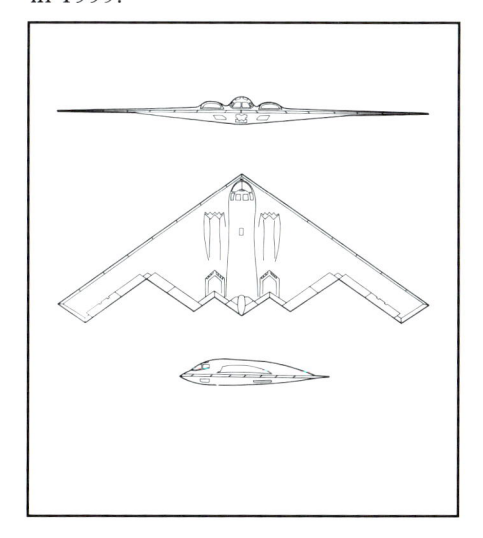

B-2A is a costly but potentially decisive warplane

B-2A Spirit

INDEX

A
Avro
  504 44
  Lancaster 47, 48
  Manchester 48
  Vulcan 52, 54

B
Bloch, Marcel 19
Boeing company 43
  B-17 Flying Fortress 45, 46
  B-29 Superfortress 49
  B-47 Stratojet 51, 53
  B-50 49, 53
  B-52 Stratofortress 53, 58
  F/A18 Hornet 9, 38
  Model 464 53
  XB-15 46
Boeing (McDonnell Douglas)
  F-15 Eagle 36, 43
British Aerospace 42

C
Canadair CF-5 30
Caproni Ca 32 44
Carter, President 58
CASA SF-5 30
Consolidated company 50
  B-24 Liberator 46
Convair
  B-36 'Peacemaker' 14, 50
  B-58 Hustler 57
  F-102 Delta Dagger 20
  F-106 Delta Dart 20

D
Dassault
  M.D. 450 Ouragan 19
  Mirage III/5 26, 35, 41
  Mirage F1 35
  Mirage 2000 41
  Mystère 19
De Havilland
  D.H.100 Vampire 13, 17
  D.H. 113 13
  D.H. 115 13
Douglas XB-19 46

E
English Electric Lightning 25, 28

F
Fairchild company 24
Falklands War 54

G
General Dynamics company 43
  F-111A 34
  Model 401 37
General Electric F-120 43
Gloster Meteor 9, 10, 11, 18
Gotha bomber 44
Grumman
  F-14 Tomcat 34
  F-111B 34

H
Halton civil transport 47
Handley Page
  O/100 43
  O/400 43
  Halifax 47
  Victor 52, 54, 56
Hawker company 11
  Hunter 18
Hiroshima, bombing of 49

I
IAI Kfir 26

K
Kolesov lift jet 32
Korean War 9, 14, 16, 23, 27

L
Lockheed company 43
  F-80 Shooting Star 9, 12
  F-104 Starfighter 9, 23, 27
  T-33 12
Lockheed Martin
  F-16 Fighting Falcon 37
  F-22 Raptor 43
Luftwaffe 9, 10

M
McDonnell Douglas
  F-4 Phantom 29, 36, 38
  F-15 Eagle 40
MAPO 'MiG'
  MiG-29 39
Messerschmitt
  Me 163 Komet 9
  Me 262 Schwalbe 9, 10, 11

Mikoyan
  MiG-15 9, 15
  MiG 17 15
  MiG-21 27
  MiG-23 32
  MiG-25 9, 31
  MiG-27 31
  MiG-29 40
  MiG-31 31
missiles
  AA-10 'Alamo' snap-down air-to-air 39
  AA-11 'Archer' 32
  AA-12 'Adder' 39
  AGM-28 Hound Dog stand-off nuclear 53
  AGM-86B ALCM 58
  AIM-9 Sidewinder air-to-air 17, 2, 23, 38, 42, 43
  AIM-54 Phoenix long-range air-to-air 34
  AIM-120 43
  AMRAAM 38, 42, 43
  anti-radar 24
  AS-3 'Kangaroo' 55
  AS-4 'Kitchen' 55
  AS-15 'Kent' cruise 55
  AS-11 'Kilter' anti-radar 31
  Aspide 23
  Avro Blue Steel stand-off nuclear 54, 56
  Firestreak air-to-air 28
  Harpoon 53
  Hughes Falcon air-to-air 25
  JDAM 58
  Mica air-to-air 42
  Red Top air-to-air 28
  Sparrow 23
  SRAM 58

N
Nagasaki, bombing of 49
NATO 23, 27, 39, 40, 55
North American
  B-70 Valkyrie 31
  F-51D Mustang 9
  F-86 Sabre 15, 16
  F-100 Super Sabre 9, 21
Northrop
  F-5 Freedom Fighter 30
  YF-17 38
Northrop Grumman
  B-2A 59

Northrop/McDonnell Douglas
  YF-23 43

O
Oerlikon-Bührle cannon 33

P
power plant systems
  Allison 12, 14
  Armstrong Siddeley 18, 22, 25, 26, 54, 56
  BMW 10
  Bristol 47, 48
  Bristol Siddeley 28, 54
  de Havilland 11, 12, 13, 17
  General Electric 12, 14, 16, 23, 26, 29, 30, 37, 38, 50, 51, 57, 58, 59
  Hispano-Suiza 19, 22
  Junkers 10
  Klimov 15, 39
  Kuznetsov 55
  Lyulka 32
  Packard 48
  Pratt & Whitney 19, 20, 21, 24, 33, 34, 35, 36, 37, 43, 45, 46, 49, 50, 53
  Rolls-Royce 11, 13, 15, 16, 18, 19, 22, 25, 28, 29, 47, 48, 52, 54, 56
  Rover 11
  Saturn 40
  SNECMA 19, 22, 26, 35, 41
  Soyuz 31, 32
  Tumansky 27, 31, 32
  Volvo 33, 42
  Wright 14, 23, 45, 49

R
radar systems 24, 29, 31, 32, 33, 34, 36, 39, 41, 59
RAF (Royal Air Force) 9, 11, 18, 29, 47, 54
Reagan, President 43, 58
Republic
  F-84 Thunderjet 14
  F-84F Thunderstreak 24
  F-105 Thunderchief 24
  P-47 Thunderbolt 9, 14
  RF-84F Thunderflash 14
Rockwell B-1B Lancer 58, 59
Royal Naval Air Service 44

S
SAAB
  21 17
  29 17
  35 Draken 25, 42
  37 Viggen 33, 42
  201 17
  JAS 39 Gripen 42
Sikorsky Ilya Mourometz 44
'Six-Day-War' 26
Sud-Est S.E.535 Mistral 13
Sud-Ouest S.O.4050 Vautour 22
Suez campaign 52
Sukhoi Su-27 39, 40
Supermarine company 11, 20

T
Tupolev
  Tu-95 55
  Tu-142 55
  TB series 44

U
U.S. Air Force 9, 16, 23, 29, 30, 36, 37, 40, 43, 46, 50, 51, 57, 58
U.S. Army Air Corps 45, 49, 50
U.S. Marine Corps 29
U.S. Navy 29, 34, 38
U.S. Strategic Air Command 51, 53

V
Vickers
  Valiant 52, 54
  Vimy 44
Vietnam War 24, 37
Vought F-8 Crusader 21

W
World War I 9, 44
World War II 10, 11, 12, 13, 16, 18, 19, 20, 29, 44, 45, 46, 47, 48, 49, 57

Y
Yakovlev Yak-9 9

Z
Zeppelin LZ32 44
Zeppelin Staaken R VI 44